"*The Matter of Little Losses* provides
quick-fix culture, inviting us to share and honor the gift of lament. Through her brave exploration of loss, Kang reminds us that in honoring sorrow we not only find solace but also a path to deeper communion with one another. I will be savoring the reflections it evoked in me for a long while to come."

Dr. Alison Cook, therapist and author of
The Best of You and *Boundaries for Your Soul*

"In *The Matter of Little Losses*, we are gently tended to and carried through the various ways grief affects us. Rachel Marie Kang draws on stories, art, and the power of our connections to remind us that our grief matters and that we are not alone in it. As you journey through your own losses, Kang's poetry, thoughtful reflections, and story weaving will guide you along the way. I am so grateful for this book."

Kaitlin B. Curtice, award-winning author of
Native and *Living Resistance*

"Rachel Marie Kang writes like a close friend you have known your whole life—the kind who gives you a long embrace when you've been apart for some time, the kind who holds your hand when you walk together, and the kind who knows what you're thinking about even when you haven't said it out loud. This book is a companion for each of us as we navigate life's changes—the 'ordinary instants,' as Rachel refers to them, when life flips. It is masterfully and powerfully written. Rachel's words will stick with you long after you've turned the last page."

Ginny Yurich, podcaster and founder of 1000 Hours Outside

"For the last three decades, my life has been marked by consecutive and unrelenting losses. Like trying to escape a riptide in the ocean, I feared the waves of grief would carry me beyond rescue. As it turns out, the process of grief—of big devastations and small disappointments—became the necessary and sacred work of true healing. In *The Matter of Little Losses*, Rachel Marie Kang gives light for those walking dark pathways of grief, in whatever form. She is a fellow sojourner, knowing firsthand the complexities and impossibilities of grief. Thus she resists pat answers and instead offers compassion, comfort, and true friendship on every page."

Michele Cushatt, executive coach and author of
A Faith That Will Not Fail

"Kang's poetic reflections on grief and loss are a sanctuary for those wrestling with the lingering sting of absence. Her attentiveness to such a delicate subject filled me with a profound sense of hope and camaraderie in reckoning with my own journey through grief. I highly recommend this and all of her work."

Stephen Roach, host of *Makers & Mystics* podcast and
author of *Naming the Animals*

"Grief is a country, and we're all moving there. Rachel has created a luminous guidebook for us. There is deep value in reading her wise words in preparation, as they will help you understand and support the ones you love who travel ahead of you and help you savor the life you have now. You won't find toxic optimism or sanctimonious tips from Rachel, just the quiet, clean story of one who has lived here a long time. And she shares the unfathomable secrets of this country—life can be beautiful here. Not the losses that brought us here but the living with them can be good and joyful and holy. Rachel shares the rich goodness she's found in her own grieving. Into her own story she interweaves questions for you, questions you can follow like a map to uncover your own deep and rich and meaningful life in the land of grief."

Kate Haynes Murphy, pastor of The Grove Church and
author of *Lost, Hidden, Small*

"Rachel Marie Kang is a person quickly defined as generous. She clearly desires to give of herself for the sake of others' well-being and betterment. She has a keen ear for rhythm and relationship, both in the way she constructs her sentences in their phonetically pleasing way and in the way she tunes herself to the emotional needs of her community—offering the balm and bandage of words spoken with care for each individual who listens."

Conor Sweetman, senior editor of *Ekstasis* magazine

"In *The Matter of Little Losses*, Rachel gave me permission I didn't know I needed to remember without shame the grief of being a human, and I came through on the other side feeling as if I'd shed layers of my past self I no longer need to carry but can honor instead. Her words are a mesmerizing dance, like a grand adage—slow, strong, and controlled."

Katherine N.

"Rachel invites readers to walk with her, hand in hand, as they experience their grief journeys through a new lens. Through sharing intimate reflections and personal stories, Rachel will peel back the layers of your heart and whisper 'You are held.' If you are looking for a transparent, healing, and redemptive exploration of grief, look no further."

Kristin A.

"Rachel writes on some of the deepest and most difficult pains and pangs, griefs and losses, with such tenderness, compassion, and gentleness that this book feels like an exercise in sitting still and breathing carefully and slowly. She reminds us there is grace beneath, and among, and despite."

Eunice H.

"This book spoke to me in the spaces, commas, and questions. Its words gave me permission to hope and heal. Grief touches all of us—but this book reminds us we can flourish and grow amid our lament."

Neidy H.

"Rachel's gift for crafting words that matter takes the reader to a sacred place, a holy space that allows the heart to soak in the truth that yes, our pain matters. Yes, there is darkness, but light burns brighter."

Ruth P.

"Rachel has a way of captivating her audience with her gut-wrenching words and deep emotion. Her work gives us a sense of hope and nostalgia and helps us embrace what's here now."

Shay C.

"*The Matter of Little Losses* is permission to feel and process our grief, to acknowledge its magnitude, its effect, and our shared human experience in our broken world. No loss is too small to be considered, and no grief is too large to be addressed head-on. I found my fears and sorrows touched tenderly, held, examined, and allowed to breathe. My griefs were given weight and looked at with the lenses of light and hope but not coddled or turned into a vacuous Sunday school lesson."

Cindy C.

"In a culture that tries to keep the realities of grief hidden in the dark and at times shames and dismisses certain types of grief, Rachel's words shine like a healing light. I felt Rachel's poetic and warm words wrap themselves tenderly around my heart. This book ushered in a new healing wave to my own lifelong grief journey."

Kristin V.

THE
MATTER
OF
LITTLE
LOSSES

THE MATTER OF LITTLE LOSSES

Finding Grace to Grieve
the Big (and Small) Things

RACHEL MARIE KANG

Revell

a division of Baker Publishing Group
Grand Rapids, Michigan

Published by Revell
a division of Baker Publishing Group
Grand Rapids, Michigan
RevellBooks.com

Printed in the United States of America

Library of Congress Cataloging-in-Publication Data
Names: Kang, Rachel Marie, 1989– author.
Title: The matter of little losses : finding grace to grieve the big (and small) things / Rachel Marie Kang.
Description: Grand Rapids, Michigan : Revell, a division of Baker Publishing Group, [2024] | Includes bibliographical references.
Identifiers: LCCN 2023018732 | ISBN 9780800740870 (paper) | ISBN 9780800745684 (casebound) | ISBN 9781493444816 (ebook)
Subjects: LCSH: Bereavement—Religious aspects. | Grief—Religious aspects. | Grace.
Classification: LCC BL65.B47 K354 2024 | DDC 204/.42—dc23/eng/20231004
LC record available at https://lccn.loc.gov/2023018732

Language of flowers in epigraphs is provided by Jessica Roux, *Floriography: An Illustrated Guide to the Victorian Language of Flowers* (Kansas City: Andrews McMeel Publishing, 2020).

Illustrations by Olivia Stallmer
Interior design by Jane Klein

Baker Publishing Group publications use paper produced from sustainable forestry practices and post-consumer waste whenever possible.

24 25 26 27 28 29 30   7 6 5 4 3 2 1

For you,
who feels grief, fights grief, fears grief

A Poem of Dedication

Here,
a flower.

For every little way
your faith fractured.

For every dream
that died, unseen.

For every friendship
failed and fallen.

For every grief
held in another's
disbelief.

For you,
a page, a place
to pour out pain.

Here's columbine,
for you, and you.

Watch the way it bends,
it moves. It dances,
delicate, though
it's drowned.

It holds,
like hope. It
lifts its head.

Resilience
makes a fool
of death.

CONTENTS

PART ONE   ITS MATTER: REFLECTIONS *ON* GRIEF

PART TWO IT MATTERS: REFLECTIONS *FOR* GRIEF

RESOURCES FOR REFLECTION: FLOWERS FROM RACHEL

FOREWORD

I met Rachel Marie Kang in the spring of 2019 in a coffee shop in Charlotte, North Carolina, right as my mind was resisting what my body already knew. My husband and I had moved to Charlotte to help pastor a church, but for the second time pastoring came with the hammer of hurt. That day, I knew I had met a kindred spirit. I didn't know I had met a doula for the deaths in my life, a friend whose kind and loving voice would echo strength across the continent after we moved back to Colorado to rebuild our lives and write our griefs into goodness in poetry and prose.

The promise of this book is not the removal of your pain but the possibility of life that emerges in reverencing it. Flower by flower, Rach teaches a return to reverencing that which society has taught us to shove away. In these pages, she offers herself to you as she has to me—as a witness to your wounds.

It takes courage to let someone witness your wounds and weariness and wariness. To let your tears be witnessed is to allow them to be planted, like seeds of future hope. As you find your way into the landscape of your losses with Rachel's words, I want you to consider the following:

What if we saw our grief as gardening?

Yesterday I knelt in the dirt of the yard of our very first house to plant columbines. I lugged a bag of soil over to the fence and carried potted plants in blue and burgundy to a place I knew the sun would stretch her warmth into their nourishment. My hand held a brand-new trowel to the earth while my heart held the old wound of hope decayed.

There's a picture of me and my husband on our first church staff retreat over a decade ago—a blue columbine, our state flower, rests in double exposure over the two of us on a mountain hike. I see our innocence, our trust that the place we'd chosen to plant our faith would nourish us into strength. That innocence died with the darkness of dominance. And when we resigned from that church, I wasn't sure we'd ever be able to find our way home again.

They say columbine stands for folly, its petals curved like a court jester's hat. And I know the angle of foolishness, the ache of thinking I was wise when really I was just leaving my body's instincts and insight behind. But they also say that columbine is for courage. *Columba*, the Latin root of columbine, means "dove"—with five petals shaped like doves in a circle of color. So as I stooped, I also prayed—planting my pain into the peace of being encircled by love. I sank my fingers into damp soil, noticing the detritus of plants long dead, and I breathed all that had decayed in me into the dark holes that would hold the beauty that was to come.

I know that like these columbines, our folly and faithlessness can become fortitude. And having been nourished by the words in this book, I know our sorrow becomes the sacred seed of hope.

K. J. Ramsey, trauma therapist and author of
The Book of Common Courage

AUTHOR'S NOTE

Grief undulates, slips thin like air in and through heart, body, and soul. It moves unnamed, unknown. A fleeting thing that is, for better or worse, forever here to stay.

What this book does not do—and what I could never do—is attempt to put a definitive grasp on grief. Grief cannot be quantified; it swells and looms large, only to shrivel and hide when sought out and sized. Grief is one thing to one person and presents a whole new face to another. It is emotion and embodied; it is expressed and it emits. It is body, spirit, mind, and soul. Hidden and seen. Felt and perceived.

It is no *one* thing, for it is everything and everywhere all at once. It is in and around me. And—whether you feel it, fight it, or fear it—grief is in and around you too.

For those of us wading through the overwhelming waves of grief, as well as those of us only just now stepping toward its shallow shores, stories will be our safest, surest way forward. Words spun into sentences spun into worlds offer witness—the most palpable and practical way to see and to be seen. This book reaches to enfold with an invitation to explore loss through the lens of literature, through stanzas and stories, through poems, and through the visual arts.

"Stories are medicine," writes psychoanalyst and poet Dr. Clarissa Pinkola Estés.[1] They are "remedies for repair" that require nothing of us but that we listen and, by leaning into the construct of characters on a page or stage, learn to approach and appreciate the stories that are our own.

As you read this book, you will encounter quotes from fiction and plays and references to art and film, all of which intend to give face and form to the ubiquitous and ambiguous nature of grief. We need levity, we need beauty, we need hope. Books can be that. Art can offer that.

It is just as professor Karen Swallow Prior, author of *On Reading Well*, writes:

> Literature embodies virtue, first, by offering images of virtue in action and, second, by offering the reader vicarious practice in exercising virtue.[2]

Irrevocably, story is embedded with the virtues we pine to embody. In reading (or telling, hearing, witnessing) story, we are afforded the safety and space to practice these virtues. Surely, stories are a kind of simulation for life—a way to participate, by way of projection, and therefore prepare us for life's curiosities, complexities, and conflicts.

I wrote about this in my book *Let There Be Art*.

> This is why movie theaters will always hush gathered hearts by the millions. This is why crowds of people will always sit before widescreens. They enjoy the thrill of watching their favorite characters live out the kind of love and loyalty they wish for themselves. It's because stories touch us deep inside, telling us what we hope for and want to believe in. It isn't futile and it isn't fruitless to be fascinated with fiction in the way that you are. It isn't weird and it isn't a waste of time to fall in love with the characters in books you read or the shows you watch. These characters are teaching you something about loss, about love. They are teaching you something about living in light and pushing back the dark.[3]

This is what led me in my undergraduate years to study English and creative writing, electing to take on classes about the modern novel, fiction writing, short stories, global literature, and literary criticism. I have always believed, with everything I know and am, that stories save lives.

Stories can light the dark and lead us home, even when nothing else has or no one else can. That is why, in dreaming up this book, I knew the only way I could write about the gravity of grief was to do so by telling you stories—ushering in beauty and balm. It was essential, *inevitable*, to integrate art into the argument of this book—to dare look death in the face through story.

Inescapable to me was the thought of unraveling fictional narratives and penning poems, offering a creative catering of comfort to soothe those interior places that, perhaps, have never received it before. In this book, you will come across reflective questions and stanzas set between sentences. You will find chapters filled with fictional characters and chapters filled with reflections on faith. You will encounter poems and prompts inviting you to exhale at the end of chapters—a sort of selah, a fragrant breath to meet you and keep you. My hope is that these poetic pauses help you open your heart to feel all that stirs within. These moments are meant to give a gracious space for all the ways your own story might encompass grief.

Reading and reflecting on loss might not come easy. You might feel tears gathering in your eyes or sense your breath becoming small and shallow. Tread gently, if and when this happens, and remember to listen to your body. Notice and name any emotions that rise to the surface. *Fear. Frustration. Annoyance. Sadness. Guilt. Resentment. Jealousy. Rage.* There is space for every feeling, however hard it may be to hold.

I hope you highlight this book. I hope you scribble messy notes in the margins and rip out pages to post on the fridge. I can already see your tears and coffee stains on these pages, painting a beautiful mosaic of the faith it took to feel your way through grief.

As these stories unravel, do all you need to do to let your soul untangle. Take breaks and move your body. Breathe and offer up prayers for all that feels broken. Skip whole chapters, rage through the pages in your journal, *yell at the sky*. Talk it through with your therapist, call a friend and cry, whisper it to your plants when you step outside and feel the sun on your face. These things will help you ground yourself in the truth: you are safe, and hope is real even though life is hard.

There will be moments when you'll see your story reflected in mine, moments when you feel as though your grief is noticed and named. And, because loss looks like many things, moments when you don't. You might wonder how or why I spoke into one facet of your loss but not another. You might be left wanting, wishing I'd shared more deeply or widely. In these moments, I hope you welcome the gentle invitation that whispers, *There is space for your story too.* I might not know all there is to your story—all you've loved and lost along the way—but I know there's space for you to name the nuances *you* know to be true.

———

My favorite thing about writing this book was, as you'll later see, exploring loss through a framework of the language of flowers. Flowers have always been offered in light of loss. Before advancements in the art of embalming bodies, flowers were also a practical solution to shroud the odors of decomposition. In and through history, flowers have been used to decorate graves—an ancient practice carrying a plethora of purposes, from honoring cultural rituals to giving flowers as rewards with a loved one for their afterlife. Flowers have also served, and still serve, as a way of sending and sharing sympathetic sentiments. In loss and death, flowers flourish where words fail, offering consolation, comfort, and the conveyance of hope.[4]

In the Victorian era, flowers became instruments of sentiment, not only in death but also in life. Jessica Roux, author and illustrator of *Floriography: An Illustrated Guide to the Victorian Language of Flowers*, writes, "The Victorian language of flowers—also called floriography—emerged as a clandestine method of communication at a time when etiquette discouraged open and flagrant displays of emotion."[5]

Flowers speak through their petals, their properties, and their poisons—from bluebells that bow in humble submission to thorny thistles that threaten your touch. Through image and metaphor, they show and tell what we know to be true of life.

There is beauty
though our
lives know
brevity.

Unimaginable
glory beyond
the truth of
our mortality.

I thought the best way for this book to examine grief was to embody it. For that reason, you'll find that some chapters hold more questions than answers. You will not find me tying things up with trite or trendy sayings. Some chapters wax heavy while others wane lighter, and references to faith and Scripture are sometimes few and far between. I open my heart unreservedly in this book, telling honest stories and telling on myself, confessing that, when in grief's grip, it is not always God we grasp and grope for. We reach, desperately stretching long our souls, in search of solace. We hold our holy hands out for one hundred things to fill them, though we know—deep down—there is but one thing we really want and need.

We want to know, irrevocably, that it *all* matters—every big and tiny thing. We want to know we are seen, believed, and beloved. We'd wait our whole lives just to see the truth written in the sky: grief is a galaxy made up of a trillion burning stars. And to lose just one star would make our world dim darker. We'd know it; we'd feel it.

And so, I hope this book reads like a letter, telling you all the things you've been waiting to hear but thought you never would. Take these words and take these stories. Read my heart on these pages and research my references to art as you, slowly and safely, explore the landscape of your losses.

Return to your own story, holding up candles to find your way out of the dark, long night. Pen your own poems as you come across mine. Reflect on the prompts and respond to the discussion questions in the back of the book. Ponder always your resilient capacity for hope and the greater story from which it stems, roots reaching deep into the dusty, ancient earth.

May this book bring you to breathe again, from every page to every poem; may it help you cradle compassion for the ones carrying boulders and stones that do not weigh like your own. May you inhale and exhale, finding a kind and momentary pause to process all you feel and fight and fear, from every pain to every pent-up dream to every death and little loss laced in between.

All,

Rachel Marie Kang

Rosemary, *Salvia rosmarinus*
Meaning: Remembrance

VISITATION

Rosemary for Remembrance

There's rosemary, that's for remembrance. Pray you, love, remember.

Ophelia (William Shakespeare, *Hamlet*)[1]

I wonder if you know the secret of time travel like I do.

Like I can sit here, unbudging on a bare rug, looking strained into a framed sheet of silver-backed glass and going back years, some decades back, to that one cruel moment when life deeply broke me.

A swell of ocean pools in my eyes. I lean in close to the mirror and my memory takes me there, to that room with a casket and one hundred gawking, teary eyes. Someone, I can't remember who, motions for me to come. They want to cradle me from crumbling, want to hold me as I hold my breath. I am nine years old and crying because I do not yet know how to share air with a lifeless body unbreathing before me.

It's my grandmother, or what appears to be her. I stare; her face looks foreign and yet so familiar. I wait, listening for the cackle of her laugh, for the bangle of bracelets always adorning the length of her arm. But there is no sound, nothing of the woman I once knew. My world waxes heavy, looms large with incurable questions that swell and surge. Just days ago, my grandmother slept in her bed, in her house beneath those tall trees, that foyer thick with the fog of incense I'll never forget.

Now she is gone.

Not a word, not a sound, not here and not ever coming back.

I never did leave her funeral, that day in May in 1998. All these years I've been standing there, wading through the waves of wonder, pondering reality, the uncalculated reason seven billion people come to life and only live to lose all the things that matter most. I've been standing there, still, after all this time, weeping through the weight of grief's gravity, the way it pulls like a clenched center, a hold on humanity—the gnawing sense of dread it gives in moments of its own choosing, whether we're ready for it or not.

"Life changes in the instant," writes Joan Didion. "The ordinary instant," she repeats throughout her gut-wrenching memoir on grief, harping on both the brevity of life and the inevitability of loss.[2]

In an instant, life as I knew it changed when my grandmother died, all those years ago. It changed again when my aunt died, when her heart just froze and stopped beating; it changed when my parents divorced; changed when I moved once, twice, three times. Life is still changing, all my compounded losses confounding me still.

Just now, in writing this and searching the internet for pictures of what used to be my grandmother's house, I've come to find that the house no longer exists. Years ago, it was demolished and built over with some 5,349-square-foot religious center. An investment property, purchased, says Google. The words on my screen seem so sanitized, formal. Wasn't it always supposed to be our memory? The house with deer and chipmunks in the big backyard. Wasn't it always supposed to be my grandmother's house with the kind neighbor handing us homegrown tomatoes over the fence?

In the ordinary instant, the house is gone; the tall trees it hid beneath and the foyer with the fog of incense, all gone. Gone, too, and quickly fading are memories of my grandmother—every flashback of her and her bangle bracelets, her breath.

Think of a time when life changed in an instant. What did you hear and what did you see? What did you lose and what did/do you feel?

This is a shattering the soul knows well, this cycle of life and love giving way to loss. We are, all of us, vulnerable to the wreckage, hearts trembling at the truth of our finitude, as well as that which we hold most dear—people, places, dreams, and things.

> Grief is a thread
> in the tapestry
> of Man,
>
> a lace of
> loss that
> knits us
> together
> where we
>
> s t a n d.

Grief comes to us in all shapes, knocking down doors of all sizes, the unanticipated guest that it is. We lose life, lose livelihood. Dreams die and bodies deteriorate with disease. Wedding bands go missing and houses fold in foreclosure. We hold our breath waiting for the bad news, waiting to hear that the world will be ripped from under our feet. We, all of us, cradle unnamed grief, crying into corners when the world isn't looking as we wait for someone—anyone—to say it's not too much to want to make sense of it all.

Sometimes when I think about my losses—all those little and large—I imagine myself standing on the edge of a vast graveyard. In this projection, I am alone. I wear black. I sound the procession. I shovel the soil, cup the cold earth in my hands. I throw the dirt on the grave at this funeral, mourning the way things were and were never supposed to be. It's like I'm standing there waiting to hear all the things I've needed to hear but never did. That it's okay to cry, okay to name my losses and lay metaphorical flowers on the graves and grounds of all things dead and gone.

What I want for myself is also what I want for you. I want to ask you, with all the words in the world, if you know the name of that pain you've left buried. I want to meet you on these pages, whisper between the lines, telling of my losses—and yours—making space for sorrow, for every shared grief.

In retrospect, when my flashbacks take me to that one funeral, there is an inescapable truth that glitters, almost like a thread of thin gold: *I was not alone.* I see myself standing there, surrounded by men and women, and I see their tears and tissues alongside my own. I see my mother, my father, holding their own tears and showing me I wasn't the only one with grief in my grasp that day.

Someone, I can't remember who, motions for me to come. They want to cradle me from crumbling. They want to hold me as I hold my pain. They want to hold me as they hold their own.

They want to hold me even while they hurt and heave, want to tell me what they know and hope to be true. That it'll be all right, that I'll be all right. All will be held. All will be well.

What thoughts, memories, images, or feelings rise to the surface when you think about funerals? What story do these memories or thoughts tell?

It takes bravery to be here, to open a book that you know will beckon you to stand at the edge of things buried beneath. All things feared and all things dead. It takes courage to come, even if only curious, crawling in uncertainty to hold a candle to all that grieves you. To open this book is to open your beating heart to the truth that you have known all along. The truth that loss, indeed, outlines love. It always has. It always will.

There is something I must tell you as you turn the pages in this book, these thin wisps of words and wonder awakening you to layers of loss interwoven with love.

It's this: I will not twist your arm and tell you to tame what is eternally torn within you, will not whisper secrets in the wind nor list the top ten ways for getting over grief. This is no guide. There is no getting over grief, no getting behind or above or beyond it.

It is everything and everywhere all at once.

There is only reminding you that **you are not alone**, that you are cradled even

It takes bravery to be here, to open a book that you know will beckon you to stand at the edge of things buried beneath.

as you crumble. There is only whispering last words of remembrance, words that give space to notice your narrative. There is visiting the graves you grieve on and standing with you.

We can return to our stories and ritualize remembrance. We can think back and travel in time; we can name the nuance, though we are gaping wide with loss and at a loss for words. Here we all are, naked and exposed, vulnerable to knowing and loving, all while holding our breath for the moments we lose the things—the ones— that matter. These things that break, the hearts that ache, the dreams that die, the lands that burn.

> We don't just need
> tissues for tears.
>
> We need words
> for wounds,
>
> language
> for loss.

Embedded in my memory forever is that moment in *Hamlet* when Ophelia, the queen's maid and Hamlet's lover, uses flowers to portray the gravity of her grief. More about this later, but Ophelia, in all her madness, demonstrates a moment of mourning with a ritual of remembrance. After all this time, having first read *Hamlet* years ago, I finally know why it captivated me.

It's the exactness of Ophelia's expression, her slant but sincere naming of very precise pains. Especially in a time and place where to do such was not at all permitted:

> There's rosemary, that's for remembrance. Pray you, love, remember. And there is pansies, that's for thoughts. . . . There's fennel for you, and columbines. There's rue for you, and here's some for me; we may call it herb of grace o' Sundays. O, you must wear your rue with a difference. There's a daisy. I would give you some violets, but they withered all when my father died.[3]

Ophelia names a flower for every sentiment, giving space for every sorrow. It isn't a rush toward restoration or resolution—it's a moment of reckoning. It's a moment in which she returns to her story and recognizes the ruin and rage, the regret and grief. I wonder, might we find relief in doing the same?

May we return to and remember, say the things we never before had the space or courage to say. May we look to our tapestries of grief and see that **love is still the strongest thread**.

Together, I'll lead you in this. Through poems, I'll put flowers to precise pains in each chapter. I will offer an empathic presence, providing prompts and a place for the profane and giving language to loss. Telling you just how much it all matters to remember. Eternally, just how much you matter too.

Here, a poem,
words to water
the ground,
the graves you
grieve on.

Find that you
face your
fear of
feeling.

Find that you
let your lungs
keep breathing.

Of your pain,
go gently
to the grave,
with rosemary, here,
memories dare
you.

For you,
flowers for
your funerals.

All those
few and far
and in between.

Remember

- Grief comes to us in all shapes.
- It takes bravery to be here.
- You are not alone.
- Love is still the strongest thread.

Reflect

- Think of a time when life changed in an instant. What did you hear and what did you see? What did you lose and what did/do you feel?
- What thoughts, memories, images, or feelings rise to the surface when you think about funerals? What story do these memories or thoughts tell?

Respire

- Inhale: I can return.
- Exhale: I can remember.

Part One

ITS MATTER

REFLECTIONS *ON* GRIEF

Marigold, *Tagetes*
Meaning: Grief

MARIGOLD

for Grace

You care so much you feel as though you will bleed to death
with the pain of it.

Professor Dumbledore (J. K. Rowling,
Harry Potter and the Order of the Phoenix)[1]

There is a cry in the world, a seething cry that cuts through
all layers of the earth, which I cannot soothe—for I am
but a notion, some unanchored thought in the heart of my
father, in the still-swollen womb deep within my mother.

He is a mere four months old when he first foams at the mouth,
baby bones rattling like a railroad track shouldering the weight of a
freight train, synapses shooting electrical explosions into gray matter
like lightning on the skeletons of trees.

He breaks
before I'm
barely , , ,
breathing.

I come into the world one year after he does, and I grow tall into a toddling, talking thing. My machine lips rage, tossing words and spewing wonder, pulling the big world up in whirls of inquisitive breaths only to hurl them long and deep into parent ears.

My parents tell me it was a needle plunging fresh into newborn flesh, that the vaccine was a vacuum that sucked dry every dream they ever held for him—my brother, the one whose body broke before I was born. They explain it to me over and over, but it never sinks in deep or long enough that my brother's brain is damaged. *He is different.* He'll never quite do anything as the rest of us do. They tell me it's been this way since before I was born, and that it will be this way until the day I die.

My world waxes heavy, looms large with incurable questions.

I remember the confusion, the bewilderment of never really knowing *why* my brother walked the way he walked or *why* he looked the way he looked. His crooked fingers, his drool dripping down the side of his face. These are the shards that shattered before I even came to be, the sharp-edged story in a book I've heard from my parents but never held for myself.

> He(re) is how the
> world breaks
> before my
> life begins.
>
> He(re) is my
> first loss, forever
> my greatest
> grief.

Loss begins at birth, all burned and branded by those first few days, months, and then years. Deeper still, loss breaks in before we come breaking through, all breathing and heart beating. What is birth if not the survival of loss? In birth, we leave the place where we were formed and first found safety.

Austrian psychoanalyst and writer Otto Rank says, "All human beings suffer trauma by virtue of being born and of the inevitable, violent, physical and psychic separation we suffer at birth from our mother." Birth, our "earliest anxiety," sets forth a sort of "blueprint for all anxieties experienced later in life."[2] This is why we cradle newborn babies on naked chests. *Skin-to-skin*, they say. It's not just for breastfeeding; it's for regulating baby's breath and anxious heartbeat.[3]

Do you know your birth story, or that of a family member? What about birth stories do you believe to be hopeful? What about birth stories do you believe to be hard?

And so it is that at birth we are all thrust into trauma, into "the impact of an injury, frightening experience, or overwhelming event that exceeds [our] capacity to cope with or process what happened in a constructive way."[4] That's what trauma is. *Unwitnessed pain* is how Dr. Alison Cook describes it. And we are thrust into trauma spiritually speaking too. We inherit injury through our bloodline. **We carry the ache of our earliest ancestors**, wearing life's first loss like it is some kind of skin.

> Where is God
> in the garden
> when they fall,
> first lose it all?

"They lived in paradise. But, they lost it. That's trauma," writes rabbi and psychotherapist Tzvi Hersh Weinreb.[5] Indeed, the fall of man is the world's first trauma, the first injury, the first loss. Of the garden, we're fond of talking about guilt and sin. But what of grief and sorrow? What about the ways in which we bear it in our bones, the paradox of a paradise painted in and through with pain? There isn't one of us who doesn't feel it, doesn't taste the tangle stuck thick in our throats.

We speak of
sin and Satan
but not of
tears and
trauma.

Death is in
our DNA,
injury is
our inheritance:

life is laced
and laced
with loss.

The man and the woman are cursed, and the world as it was concaves into collapse, just as God said it would. *For you shall surely die.* And they do—in every physical, spiritual, and metaphorical sense of the word.

> I will make your pains in childbearing very severe;
>   with painful labor you will give birth to children.
> Your desire will be for your husband,
>   and he will rule over you. (Gen. 3:16)

> Cursed is the ground because of you;
>   through painful toil you will eat food from it
>   all the days of your life.
> It will produce thorns and thistles for you,
>   and you will eat the plants of the field.
> By the sweat of your brow
>   you will eat your food
> until you return to the ground,
>   since from it you were taken;
> for dust you are
>   and to dust you will return. (vv. 17–19)

God declared that humankind would dance with death. That woman would know pain amid life. Man, too, would know strife and physical death. *Until you return to the ground*, God says. Until you breathe no more, until you die.

Still, they survive, and life persists with pain. Theirs is a survival story, and it reads like a saga—seemingly endless, folding in and out of generations. We weep, always, for the hundreds of ways loss lingers in our world. The one thousand wars we wage and survive. The broken earth; our broken bodies. The holocausts, the generational sins, the murders, the addictions.

We weep, always, for the hundreds of ways loss lingers in our world.

> Loss on Eve's
> lips sings a song
> of survival, the
> same song in
> my soul. On
> living, on
> loving, on
> losing the world.
>
> Of piety,
> of pining
> for heaven,
> for home.

All the world may say what it wants to say—all the platitudes and prayers about how you still have breath in your body and life in your lungs and how thankful you can and should be and the many lessons there are to learn from surviving sorrow. Still, the world turns a kind of tortured shade. We are thrust unaware through traumas that only break us further.

To live at all is to survive loss, and to grieve loss is to deeply need grace.

What losses or sorrows have you survived or are you surviving?

There's this story about an orphan with no brothers or sisters, no one to call his own. He is born, then quickly left behind by two loving parents tragically killed. His story echoes the searing pain of survival, pain that comes to those of us who outlive the ones we love. Try as he may to live and lead life normally, he cannot, for he soon discovers his world is a broken place filled with broken people. He forever thinks of that which he cannot undo—his greatest grief and the one thousand little losses that will never leave him. He reckons he lost more than his parents' love the day they died. He lost everything he was and was to become. Little dreams, little joys, little losses all knotted together.

He was about to go home, about to return to the place where he had had a family. It was in Godric's Hollow that, but for Voldemort, he would have grown up and spent every school holiday. He could have invited friends to his house. . . . He might even have had brothers and sisters. . . . It would have been his mother who had made his seventeenth birthday cake. The life he had lost had hardly ever seemed so real to him as at this moment, when he knew he was about to see the place where it had been taken from him.[6]

But they were not living, thought Harry: They were gone. The empty words could not disguise the fact that his parents' moldering remains lay beneath snow and stone, indifferent, unknowing. And tears came before he could stop them, boiling hot then instantly freezing on his face, and what was the point in wiping them off or pretending? He let them fall, his lips pressed hard together, looking down at the thick snow hiding from his eyes the place where the last of Lily and James lay, bones now, surely, or dust, not knowing or caring that their living son stood so near, his heart still beating, alive because of their sacrifice and close to wishing, at this moment, that he was sleeping under the snow with them.[7]

While I write these words they take me down memory lane to the years when I, a young girl, glorified the heroism of Harry Potter. I admired the book series for its sense of adventure, and I celebrated the characters and their hard-won victories, missing, entirely, the core narrative that connects Harry Potter to myself and the millions of others who bought the books.

He is orphaned so young. He survives what should have killed him. For this, he cradles a grief that needs grace.

Harry Potter books have sold by the millions not merely because we dream of defeating wizards but because we see our losses reflected in Harry's life. Like Harry, we see the deaths and gaping grief, but we also feel the sting of "little" things. *The home we might have had. The friends we might have had. The candles on birthday cakes we might have had.* All knotted up with what the world sees as the only "obvious" grief: death.

This is what we need space for; *this* is why we need grace. We need permission to speak of and scream out these things. We need room to breathe and a place to grieve. We need allowance and acknowledgment. We need confession without condemnation.

Harry Potter's tears came "before he could stop them." In what moments of loss have you tried to stop your tears?

I wonder how long your loss has lingered, when it started, and where it began. In the hospital room, or on a battlefield in a far-off country? I wonder if you know your grief is twofold. There is the tragedy of loss and the trauma of life. There is the love you lost and the change that came after. I wonder about the horrors you have survived. Who have you loved and outlived? What incurable changes have come and shaken your world? The jabs of needles, the infants heir to one thousand horrors. The gunshots that rang out under streetlights all those years ago, while you hid beneath blankets in that apartment off Lenox Avenue.

Loss is like a leaky hole always dripping, incessantly, quietly, consistently there. It reframes our focus and traumatically changes our name. We see it every day in the smallest of ways. **We cradle grief because we care.** It matters. Everything small and tugging about it matters. Not just the loss of life but of every small, unspoken dream—going to college, creating the cure, wondering about all the many ways their face might have taken shape and form in age, through all the years to come.

The challenge becomes finding help for what haunts. How do we live and breathe and be all that we still need to be?

> How do we survive
> through sorrow?
> How do we live
> through loss?

Keiko Ogura was eight years old when the atomic bomb fell through the sky on August 6, 1945, landing in Hiroshima and instantly killing 80,000 of the city's 350,000 people. She is a *hibakusha,* a survivor of atomic bombs. Along with other survivors, she tells her story about seeing a big flash in the sky and people dropping to the ground, a whole city dying before her eyes. *Hibakusha* talk to share their truth and the truth of what happened that day, in hopes that atomic bombs never happen again.[8]

Haunted by the memories, they still hope that no other bombs, weapons of mass destruction, take lives . . . like they once did in the blink of an eye. They tell their stories of survival so that there don't have to be other survivors, so that they can be the last of the *hibakusha.* "People like me wondered why they had lived when so many others had died," says Ogura. "I could never forget the two people who died in front of my eyes. But I will keep talking about what happened until my last breath, so that they and the other victims did not die in vain."[9]

They wake and they walk, even with the shrapnel of explosions—those bombs that fell from the sky to blow up all constructs of belief, their thoughts about safety, control, and calm.

How does knowing that the hibakusha, *survivors of atomic bombs, tell their stories of surviving loss speak to you?*

It is me waking and walking with the shrapnel of explosions in my story too. It is me fostering fear for the future and wondering how to live through my scary tomorrows without fearing the repeat of my yesterdays.

We want normal; we want life unscathed, without scratch and without scar—like we have any kind of control over the heat of the sun-scorching or the erosion of banks of sand, worn away by relentless waves. What we want is to live life blissfully unaware of any kind of "before," any kind of preceding standard that might set the stage for forever's tomorrows.

But yesterday cannot be erased, nor can its losses. Deep within, what we want is to rise above what we cannot unknow and unsee. We want life before the seizures, the addiction, and putting down the pets. Life the way things could and should have been.

We need grace for grief, space to spill it out free and unfiltered. Like Harry, finally releasing all his buried grief and letting it rage raw, as he rips through Professor Dumbledore's office with the honest truth: "'I DON'T CARE!' Harry yelled. 'I'VE HAD ENOUGH, I'VE SEEN ENOUGH, I WANT OUT, I WANT IT TO END, I DON'T CARE ANYMORE—'"

But Professor Dumbledore replies, "You do care." Knowing grief and knowing Harry, he insists, "You care so much you feel as though you will bleed to death with the pain of it."[10]

Yes, admit it—it hurts. Confess how it hurts that your heart still beats though theirs doesn't. Confess that you long to cry despite how long ago it happened. Confess that you are knee-deep in grief because you care . . . it's always been because you cared.

I see
marigolds in
your midst.

Burning blood,
opulent orange.

Petals carried
by the wind.

Broken heart
and mind to
mend.

———

Just because
you survived
doesn't mean
it didn't scar you.

———

Here is rue,
for you
for all you
can't undo.

Willow for all the
ways you weep,
the tears of day
and tears of sleep.

And asphodel,
for how you feel
you failed
and fell.

Azalea for the
ache of heart,
snowdrop as you
now depart.

Walking on toward
a better day,
hold on to hope,
love, this I pray.

42

Remember

- Loss begins at birth.
- We carry the ache of our earliest ancestors.
- To live at all is to survive loss.
- We cradle grief because we care.

Reflect

- Do you know your birth story, or that of a family member? What about birth stories do you believe to be hopeful? What about birth stories do you believe to be hard?
- What losses or sorrows have you survived or are you surviving?
- Harry Potter's tears came "before he could stop them." In what moments of loss have you tried to stop your tears?
- How does knowing that the *hibakusha*, survivors of atomic bombs, tell their stories of surviving loss speak to you?

Respire

- Inhale: There is grace.
- Exhale: I can grieve.

Daffodil, *Narcissus*
Meaning: Unrequited love

DAFFODIL
for Love

Some people build fences to keep people out . . . and other people build fences to keep people in. Rose wants to hold on to you all. She loves you.

Bono (August Wilson, *Fences*)[1]

I watch kaleidoscopic colors twirl and toss explosions under the covering of a big top, listening to the euphoric echo of laughter billowing out like waves across water. We are bedazzled by the circus, our eyes playing tricks on our minds as we watch the blazing fire and crazy clowns, the people flying and tiptoeing in midair.

It is a magical spectacle, lodging a reel of photographic memories, which intermittently show themselves like dreams that will forever linger and stay. I smile, bend a reminiscent curve on my face, only to let it fall and fade at the realization of what this circus really signifies for me.

That life with a brother with brain damage *is* a circus.

It is every breathtaking, jaw-gaping spectacle, a show that brings as much mayhem as merriment, as much fear as folly. There are always loops to go around, ambiguous holes and hoops to circumvent. There is the perpetual changing of diapers, always gymnastic. The bending under and the stooping over, the stretching of arms across big spaces.

There is the balancing act, the tactful tossing and catching of appointments; prescription pickups; meetings with teachers, lawyers, accountants, doctors, doctors, and more doctors. Then there is juggling us other children and our lives too.

My body encodes the chaos of it all, stills at the sight of my brother seizing, his head hitting the floor. My heart pounds; my mind makes memories of the many piles of washcloths and pillowcases soaked through with blood from the nosebleeds, the busted lips. Always, I hear echoes of things. A pandemonium of voices and violent convulsions, his tonic-clonic cry and "Turn him on his side," my parents saying, seemingly one hundred times.

What is a circus without an audience? We have that too. At this circus, the crowds do not applaud. Instead they stand appalled with frowning faces, watching my brother limp and stutter and drool. Strangers stop and stare in public places, gawking with mouths wide open, looking long enough to let us know that they know.

He is different.

He'll never quite do anything as the rest of us do.

All of this hammering heavily into the heart of a little girl. Like a tightrope of tension, she tiptoes around sorrow and shame, the guilt and the grief. Her circus is a shattered show, isn't all popcorn and cotton candy. Beneath this big top, hearts break easy.

What kind of memories or metaphors come to mind when you think back to your childhood? Do you see a circus? Do you see chaos or calm?

Life is like a circus, a chaotic cascade of act after act, all falling in and out and from one another. It is a juggling of the jaded and the jarring, a taming of wild and dangerous animals—all under lock and key in the same cage, under the same roof, between the same thin walls. Exhilarating and frightening all in the same breath.

> There is the beautiful
> and the bright.
>
> There is the broken
> and the night.

My parents divorced just before I reached middle school and, though I knew I didn't cause their parting, I always wondered what did. Was it the chaos of our family's circus or the heartbreak of my brother's story? Was this just life, calamity after catastrophe? Was it decades of stacked stories and sorrows? *My uncle lost to leukemia. My father's father killed in the line of duty.* Loss, it seems, is that constant thread laced irrevocably through love and life—that paradox of pain in paradise.

An article I see on the National Library of Medicine's website catches me with its title: "The Impact of Family Structure on the Health of Children: Effects of Divorce." In it, loss, as evaluated by experts researching the experiences of children of divorced parents, is listed like a litany.

The child may lose time with each parent.

The child may lose economic security.

The child may lose emotional security.

The child may have decreased social and psychological maturation.

The child may change his or her outlook on sexual behavior.

The child may lose his or her religious faith and practice.

The child may lose cognitive and academic stimulation.

The child may be less physically healthy.

The child may have a higher risk of emotional distress.[2]

Isn't it like the truth to ring loud in retrospect, telling me what I never learned but knew in my bones all along? Divorce is a death that digs deeply, daily. It is an amputation that hollows a hole of ambiguous loss, the kind of "unresolved loss that 'complicates grief and confuses relationships.'"[3] It comes in under cover, slips in like a sweep of wind, a draft undetected beneath the door. It lays low and lingers long, until it is layers thick and tells the story of its tattered pieces.

I am not the only one who knows the loss of love, not the only one who ever felt the impact of someone else's lost love. It is my parents who suffered loss when their love was lost. It's the engagements that end, the breakups that burn all memories away, the kin that cut you off, the estrangement that stings still. It is the slow trickle of one million relentless reminders that life has been changed, forever ripped from the heart.

The lines blur, bleeding one into another until we don't know what is hurting—until we only know that we hurt. The pain of waking up, of pushing through the days and nights, the months and years. The truth taunts us, a cruel reminder that **we cannot rule love, we can only release it**.

Have you ever lost love or felt the impact of someone else's lost love? If so, how so?

The main character of August Wilson's 1986 play (turned film), *Fences*, Troy Maxson is a broken man who cannot bear the thought of whispering that very truth with his own breath. Troy reels in the reminders of his haunted history, a life layered with losses in and through the years. He is a Black man living in the aftermath of America's freed slaves, a time and place where, though freedom was granted, systemically it was not sustained.

He is the son of a sharecropper who was "frustrated by the fact that every crop took him further into debt,"[4] the brother of a man who emerged disoriented and damaged from World War II, and he's reeling in the loss of past passions, unable to play big league baseball because of segregation. His loss is layered; it blends and bleeds, connects and compounds in all its chaos.

Troy learns, from his father, to live and lead his life through verbal abuse and violence, scaring and scarring the ones closest to him. He longs to love—to give his two sons what he never had. His sole responsibility is to teach these Black men values he knows and hopes will take them far in life. He also loves his wife, though that love comes with limits, for he is proud, insistent on his ways, obsessive about being right, vulgar, violent, controlling and compartmentalized, and unfaithful.

"I'm gonna build me a fence around what belongs to me," he yells, screaming at Death after his mistress dies from complications while giving birth to their daughter. "And then I want you to stay on the other side. See? You stay over there until you're ready for me."[5] Troy protests as if he can keep hurt and harm away from himself, as if he could live and have love on his own terms.

But Death is no respecter of persons.

But Death is no respecter of persons. Death comes when Death wills, when it wants and however it wants. Death greets Troy unmatched, takes what it wants (his mistress and ultimately his independence), and later proves that this prideful man is powerless in its grip, just like the rest of us.

For Rose, Troy's wife, the meaning of a fence is to keep close the ones she loves. Rose believes in this sentiment so much so, she speaks it to her son at the end of the play on the morning of Troy's funeral. Their son Cory, embittered by the harm caused by his father, returns home from the Marines and tells Rose he's not going to the funeral. To this, she replies:

> Boy, hush your mouth. That's your daddy you talking about. I don't want to hear that kind of talk this morning. I done raised

you to come to this? You standing there all healthy and grown talking about you ain't going to your daddy's funeral? . . . Your daddy wanted you to be everything he wasn't . . . and at the same time he tried to make you into everything he was. I don't know if he was right or wrong . . . but I do know he meant to do more good than he meant to do harm.[6]

Throughout the play, this consistent idea of a fence presents a sort of holographic symbolism, ever so slightly changing from one character's perspective to another's. It represents self-preservation and protection, love and loyalty. In the beginning of *Fences*, it represents neglect, then after Troy succumbs to Death, it presents within its perimeter a garden.[7]

This fence represents the tension that comes with togetherness. The coming and the going. The flourishing and the failing. The control and the chaos. The atrophy of affection, the loss of love. It's a circus as rich with captivating allure as it is with conflict.

A chaotic cascade of act after act, all falling in and out and from one another.

Where in your life do you notice figurative fences? Do you build fences to keep people in or to keep them out?

We cannot fence in the people we love, and we cannot fence out what we fear. We cannot control, cannot shield ourselves from the vulnerability of the inevitable. We can only unclench our fists and release our grip on grief. We can bear our fears instead of haphazardly building fences. We can lay down control and instead come face-to-face with our wounds, even our wrongs. **We can confess our weaknesses**, refusing to contain what is tender and true about ourselves. We can stand before that circus room of mirrors, the one that shapes and shifts our sight, and we can learn to see our feelings for what they really are.

50

The fear of losing love.

We are afraid we will be abandoned, afraid to give all our trust and vulnerability away. We cannot fathom the thought of letting something or someone go or, vice versa, them letting us go. So we build walls and fences to keep things in. We build walls and fences to keep people out. We stay in abusive relationships we shouldn't, we avoid relationships altogether for fear of how they'll fracture us and fall apart. We entertain the voices in our heads that teach us how to cling and control.

We hide way up on the high ropes; we cage ourselves in protective barriers to stave off our stories—the marriage that disintegrated into divorce, the family that fell away. We hurl flamethrowers, swing tired and tried from one trapeze to another. And it is scary and shocking; it's the whole startling, frightening show—but now we've closed our eyes and can't see all the other things before us that are beautiful and stunning and good.

> Who taught you
> to hold your
> broken breath?

However—and wherever—you've built fences, maybe gardens can grow? Maybe flowers *can* flourish, like daffodils pushing up through winter's harsh ground. Maybe seeds can be planted in hope and in faith.

> Space,   a moment of silence.

> For the love you gave
> but did not get back.
> For the love you grieved
> but could not get over.

Right here and now, your voice is valid. **Your loss is legitimate**, and there is compassion for you as you carry the wounds that you do. There is grace for the grief, the many ways you lost the love that gave your life meaning.

There is compassion for you as you carry the wounds that you do.

———

There was this fence in the backyard of my childhood home. I remember my father out there, driving nails into wooden beams, pouring concrete into the ground, all the many days it took to build it. I remember the safety that fence gave me, gave all of us, when we played outside, riding our bikes in the backyard and hiding between the branches of our althea bush.

What most hurts or scares you about losing love?

I think of the many losses that came to pass behind the thin walls of that house, the boundary of that fence. All the ways in which we learned to let go of the things we couldn't control.

"Do you remember Grandma's house?" my father asked. Of course I remembered. It was the one filled with the thickest layer of smoke from incense and surrounded by the tallest trees.

"We're moving into Grandma's house," he said. "A new house . . . it will give our family a new start."

His words slip through my hands like sand, leaving more questions than answers, the sure hollowing of a hole, a gentle shallowing. A numbing within.

I didn't want a new house, though. I only wanted to know why our fence couldn't keep all of us together in life, in love.

It isn't your
fault that
flowers
fall.

———

I found flowers
in the still-frozen
field, daffodils
defiant and daring
as ever. *Up*
up up they
come, through
bitter ground,
through cold,
climbing
to better
ground.

———

I am sorry your fences failed and that you could not
keep the love you longed for. I am sorry that hearts
break uneven, jagged little corners cutting halfway
through deflated lungs and cars and kids, but I am not
sorry that you loved—not sorry that life came from your
love, my life to be exact, because the loss hallowed a
hole for you, right here, a place in my heart, broke even,
forever, for you, the both of you.

———

It is the 14th of February
and we walk, beyond
the briars in our backyard,
thorns catching in our skin.
A patch of yellow enchants
our eyes, draws us closer,
daffodils, winter's flower,
birthed through frost.
We cut them down to the stem,
careful not to bend or break them
then, we leave some for the rest.

Remember

- Life is like a circus.
- We cannot rule love, we can only release it.
- We can confess our weaknesses.
- Your loss is legitimate.

Reflect

- What kind of memories or metaphors come to mind when you think back to your childhood? Do you see a circus? Do you see chaos or calm?
- Have you ever lost love or felt the impact of someone else's lost love? If so, how so?
- Where in your life do you notice figurative fences? Do you build fences to keep people in or to keep them out?
- What most hurts or scares you about losing love?

Respire

- Inhale: Love will find me.
- Exhale: Always.

Camellia, *Camellia*
Meaning: Longing for you

CAMELLIA
for Home

We're all searching for a piece of home, or a piece of ourselves.

Michelle Zauner, *Crying in H Mart*[1]

We live on the street by the one-way tunnel, the street where sneakers dangle from telephone wires like sparkling earrings. The last thirty seconds of every car ride back home, as we turn right onto our street and drive beneath the sneakers, I look up in awe, wondering how they get so high up and if there is a fairy who comes late at night, stringing those sneakers from wire to wire, hanging them ever so carefully, making sure each one looks just right.

And I believe in this fairy tale until a friend tells me those sneakers aren't tossed up high to make the streets look pretty. They aren't dangling wire to wire because some magical fairy felt like throwing a good time. I am told that those sneakers hang to mark the houses on our street where you can get your crack. Or your weed. Or your one-night stand—whatever fix you need. In an instant, I go from thinking I am living in a wonderland to understanding that, really, I could very much be in the middle of gang wars and drug deals. The only magic in it was never seeing what was really there.

When it comes time to move, we pack up the toys and the clothes; we pack up the memories, the marriage, putting everything into moving boxes. We pack up memories I hold of my first home. Of riding bikes in the backyard and on the driveway, of the tiny garden of annual flowers in the front yard. These meld with memories of long walks from my house to the park with my mother and brothers, our big Astro van of a maroon color I'll never forget.

Grandma's house is a split-level ranch, suitable for two families to live in at once. Both stories have bedrooms, a bathroom, and a kitchen. There is thick, white fur left over from my grandmother's cat. *Stromboli*. What an odd name for a cat, I always thought.

Shortly after we move, my aunt gives me a jewelry armoire, one of the tiny ones with drawers, and it is filled with gaudy jewelry, heavy golden earrings and bangles.

"These were your grandmother's," she tells me. "Now they belong to you, so take care of them." I run my fingers through the earrings, the bangles and bracelets, the pins. I tell her they're beautiful and that I'll keep them forever.

But how nice it would be if it were my grandmother I could keep forever, along with my old home, dangling sneakers and all. How nice it would be if only I could keep my old room, old school, old friends, and everything else I know and love by heart.

Engage your senses and ponder memories of your first home. What color were the walls? What was the landscape outside the windows? What spices filled the kitchen? Where did you play, cry, and laugh?

There is a grief that comes when you lose your home, and it's deeper still when you lose your homeland. It is the pain of being separated from *place*, that holding space of all you are. Like the man and the woman cast from the garden. Like a baby born into a frightening, bright world.

The loss of home leads us, like perpetual sojourners setting out, ever searching for our beginning and our belonging. Ever in search of the homes that held our first roars of laughter, those doors held open by our tiny hands, and our drawings on the walls, scribbled in secret. We even find ourselves in search of land, the precise location from which our stories stem, from which the tales of our people come, the acres that stretch wide and wild with the certitude of our family's history.

I hold an ache in the pit of my stomach when I think of the homes I've moved away from, an ache that turns and twists like a knot. I think of the houses abandoned, the towns forsaken, the memories tethered to maps, the hospitals that house our birth stories, and old backroads memorized like lines in the palm.

We can be nomads in our own narrative, can feel like a stranger in our own story, just stopping by and traveling through, forever looking for something we feel we will not and cannot ever find. This sense of placelessness has everything to do with personhood, has everything to do with the ways our lives will project forward—who we will become and why. We are, all of us, trying to go back to the backyards where we learned to throw baseballs, the kitchens where we learned how to cook.

We can be nomads in our own narrative, can feel like a stranger in our own story.

We are trying to get back to the fields our families farmed, the ancient recipes and remedies, hoping to know what we need to make the soups and sauces. We search for bloodlines lost in map lines, the immigrant story of coming to a new land only to find ourselves missing the old one. Generations stretch out, longer and farther from our place of origin, straining and stretching to hold on to who we are. But the currents of change are strong, washing it all away in the waters of time.

What do you know, or wish you knew, of your family's homeland or country of origin?

"Katrina is becoming a folktale," says Arnold Burks, "and we're the storytellers." He is a Black man with long and twisted black hair that's tied up as he is interviewed for the 2022 HBO documentary film *Katrina Babies*. Burks shares his story, along with a few other survivors of Hurricane Katrina, the 2005 hurricane that displaced approximately two hundred thousand New Orleans residents.[2]

Katrina Babies, directed by hurricane survivor Edward Buckles Jr., was created to document the unnamed and unnoticed trauma of a forgotten generation, those "who were as young as three at the time" and who recollect "losing their homes, communities, and way of life to the hurricane."[3] From the documentary's discussion guide, Buckles poses the following:

> We often look at the consequences of natural disasters in terms of numbers—number of deaths, number of homes destroyed, number of dollars cost. Less often do we look at the toll these disasters take in less measurable ways, such as the mental health of its survivors.[4]

This kind of trauma feels like a trend. It is the Indian Removal Act and our nation's failure to fully recognize all the unnamed and nuanced ways that the trauma of displacement still permeates Indigenous peoples to this day. It's the way that the loss of land brought about a loss of cultural identity, losing homelands east and west, leaving behind sacred sites, losing language, losing rights and rituals and ceremonies and traditions.[5]

It's the Mexico–United States border crisis, the tensions deepening from the tendency to quickly turn away from this problem without fully understanding the heaps of history at play, like Central America's past with Spain's control and power, which only exacerbated inequality and perpetuated poverty.[6] And what about the ways in which America continues to create conditions that welcome—no, warrant—the employment of undocumented immigration workers. "We all participate in—and profit from—an economy that relies on undocumented labor," writes associate professor Julia Young in her article "A Wall Can't Solve America's Addiction to Undocumented Immigration" in the *Washington Post.* "From the food we eat to the hotels we stay at to the built environment that surrounds us, almost no American goes a day without benefiting from the labor of undocumented immigrants," she writes.[7]

We want to put up a wall and patch all our problems without admitting the systemic consequences, brought up by systemic actions, all of which revolve around the currency of land. In our attempts to keep the wealth we've made, to not disrupt our normalcy, and to keep things stable, we continue on, rarely turning our eyes to the traumas that tell the truth of unnamed, unnoticed pain.

Pain.
Unwitnessed pain.[8]

Trauma tears
when we turn
away from a
people's pain.

There is a name for this kind of grief. It is called *disenfranchised* because it's a grief that society often dismisses, and those carrying it are deprived of the right to call their pain what it is.[9] The impact is disorienting, even years after displacement occurs, because not only is this grief often disregarded and expected to resolve quickly but it comes with a whole host of other ambiguous losses: friendship, family, culture, heritage, land ownership, wealth, and dreams for the future, all of which are critical and crucial in the formation of values, personhood, and culture.

Where is home to you? Is it a hometown or a country of birth? Why is it home to you?

Michelle Zauner, a Korean American musician and author of the bestselling memoir *Crying in H Mart*, tells her story of losing her mother to cancer. In her memoir, she explores her landscape of loss through rituals of food, seeking to encounter memories of her mother, but what she finds is that she also encounters connections to her culture. Her story is much like that of many who are searching their stories, skimming beyond the surface for something to grab hold of, something definitive and true. She writes:

> Within the past five years, I lost both my aunt and mother to cancer. So, when I go to H Mart, I'm not just on the hunt for cuttlefish and three bunches of scallions for a buck; I'm searching for their memory. I'm collecting the evidence that the Korean half of my identity didn't die when they did. In moments like this, H Mart is the bridge that guides me away from the memories that haunt me, of chemo head and skeletal bodies and logging milligrams of hydrocodone. It reminds me of who they were before: beautiful and full of life, wiggling Chang Gu honey-cracker rings on all ten of their fingers, showing me how to suck a Korean grape from its skin and spit out the seeds.[10]

She sets out to the Korean grocery store, vulnerably alone and navigating a world she is scantly acquainted with. She cradles connection to culture with care, always wondering what is the right way to make something, eat something. What is the right brand of seaweed to buy. How to cook it just so, just like Mom always did. She comes to find comfort in cooking the Korean dishes her mother once made for her, dishes that at first felt foreign but in time ultimately tethered her to her mother and her mother's motherland. She finds not only food that tastes good but food that feels good—food that heals because of all the ways it carries her back home. **Grief is a shadow stitched to story**—her story—but in the outlines and through her rituals of food, Michelle begins to see the goodness that was always inevitably there. Her story is one that resonates not only with many Korean Americans but many others—myself included—who also feel a kind of dissonance between their present and their past, their country and the culture handed to them in America. It is a perpetual loss we're ever straining to notice, to name. And yet embedded into the expedition is a reconciliation that happens as a result of the returning.

Michelle grasps through her grief and reaches to remember, to reclaim. Hers is a journey with an ebb and flow, a rise and fall, through mountains of memories disappearing just as definitely as her mother. But what she encounters, she clings to. And it carries her through, irrevocably connects her to that which she desperately longs to call her own, her home.

> I want a home
> that holds me,
> I want a land
> that knows my
>
> n a m e.

Home is a holding place not just of safety and sanctuary but story—the gathered stories of those who came before and the hopeful stories of those to come. A space to hide, a space to be held for all you are. This is the story of displaced Indigenous peoples and tribes, a story not just of mere moving or loss of land—it is a losing of where you come from and ultimately who you *are*. This is also the story of those who endured the horror of the Holocaust, the loss of leaving land intertwined with loss of life, of which repercussions of ruin still ripple to this day. This is the story of those whose homes were uprooted by hurricanes and tornadoes, and it's the story of enslaved Africans who knew the sorrow of "living in a land but never being a part of it. Living in a land and yet still straining to see the love in it. Living in a land and yet longing for a way out of it."[11]

An article from *Psychology Today*, "What If Your Home Were Suddenly Gone?," explores the devastating impact of one's loss of home, a loss that has less to do with financial loss or gain and more to do with the emotional attachment we form with our homes.

> For most people, home is more than the structure where they live. Our sense of home can also include the neighborhood, the parks, the stores, the schools and the people who make up the community. This observation explains why most people choose to rebuild rather than move away from the site of a disaster.[12]

Home also matters because, as Roni Tower writes in her article "The Meaning of 'Home,'" home is "the center for forging and nourishing human attachment bonds."[13] Home is a cradle of memory, a nest for nourishing how we come to form bonds and relationships with those we know and love and live with. Home is a foundation for our future, in more ways than one, providing identity, a place to become, and, at times, wealth. To lose your home—or to look back and realize you never really had a home to hold you—sets you into a perpetual pining for the past, all the while yearning for a future to span beyond the length of your life.

For me, the longings and loss come layered as a mixed woman whose story of descent is but a tattered quilt. I search the internet, read what books I can, attempt to hold close the stories my parents and grandparents have told me about my heritage. I try to patch together all of the pieces of this hand-me-down history, but I can't seem to stitch the seams strong enough to create a clear picture of who I am. It's a photo that dances, fleeting, across my mind—faces whose names I do not know, stories I have not heard and will never hear.

In particular, there is one part of my story that aches, seemingly always. It is the part of me I hardly utter, barely ever lead with.* I strain with this loss that feels more like a longing, a daily reminder

---

* I've spent the last few years leaning into and leading with my African American heritage, all the while never feeling the permission or freedom to explore the nuances of my Native descent. It feels like breath, trembling but refreshing, to lean into and lead with this uncharted part of my story and family. If you are curious and want to read an expression from the perspective of my African American heritage, read the chapter "Let There Be Tears" in my first book, *Let There Be Art*.

that I have to work to learn and remember my roots, work to trust that they are true and mend my soul to know they matter.

> I am a Manhattan
> mural of my own,
> a swirl of colors,
> spiraling Black
> and White and
> Indigenous gold.[14]

I am years removed and miles away from New York, my home, when I learn that the Ramapough Lenape Nation is holding a ceremony to commemorate the transfer of a 285-year-old land use deed. The deed, found in the possession of a family from Sloatsburg, New York, was returned "by its descendants to the Ramapough tribe in a symbolic ceremony."[15] The news of it brings blood rushing to my face.

I am Ramapough.

The Ramapough are my people, my stories, passed down like legends in the wind, stories spoken from my grandmother's lips and captured in candid photos. We are the ones who belong to Hillburn, that hollow in eastern New York, just there where the valley dips between the Hudson. I am told, and have learned, that we were pushed up into the Ramapo mountains. My people hid and fled for fear of being enslaved by colonial settlers. Fled for fear of losing the land. Fled to find safety, some sort of new beginning. Still, it's all a mystery, a puzzle that always seems to be incomplete without that one missing piece.

But it matters to me. It matters to know and make sense of my story in a way that feels sacred and honoring and whole. The article "The Ramapough Lunaape of New Jersey" puts it eloquently:

> The question of Ramapough identity involves making sense of the Native people who stayed in New Jersey and how they formed community with others moving through the region—which included Native Americans, Africans, and Dutch and

English settlers. The complexity of these groups encountering each other—as they were fleeing to escape colonial violence or enslavement, or to find settlement opportunities—has complicated the debate around Ramapough identity. This braided knot of encounter is not well understood through standard American frameworks of identity, which tend to focus on pure categories.[16]

There is no
blood test
to take and
tell of our
belonging.

Don't need
your vials to
vouch for
our validity.

Another instance I came across in research is a digitized clipping of a 1923 *New York Times* article, "An Indian Canoe, Perhaps 1,000 Years Old, Unearthed by Dredge in Witteck Lake, N.J." I weep because the words place a pang in my heart; my breath slows to a halt, my ribs contract, my body freezes, and tears pool in the corners of my eyes. The story opens:

Cedar bottoms, centuries old, from sunken canoes attributed to the ancient Ramapo Indians have been unearthed by dredgers from the bottom of Witteck Lake near Butler, N.J., it was learned yesterday.[17]

Moments of discovery like this, and the 285-year-old land use deed, tell me and my family what we already know and believe to be true. Moments like this hold together the hand-me-down histories we hear all through life. Legends from the lips of our grandmothers, tall tales spun by great-uncles that no doubt exaggerate but still tell the truth. As I discover this, a guarantee is etched against all guesses. I am right there, seeing that cedar canoe in my mind, wondering already the names of the ones who crafted it. *Who were they? How were they? And, What should this mean to me?*

> I wipe away tears and burn sage.
>
> Sacred sage
> burns and bends
> lifts and mends
>   my spirit.
> Twist and turn
> mourn and burn, away, at last
> to breath and ash.

I want to whisper to you the same thing I tell myself in secret, in quiet rooms behind closed doors when no one is there to tell me who I am or what to do: **you are everything you know you are**, even if by speculation and story, even if by mere memory. Whatever glimmer of gold that comes to you in those oral stories, whatever goodness you see reflected in the black-and-white photos taken before you were born—you can claim them. Keep them close to your heart, even if you cannot return to your country of origin, the place of your past, or those dusty backroads. Even if you cannot return to the small shop on the corner or shake hands with those neighbors who once knew your name.

Retrace your way home by way of ritual, by way of food, cooking your way through culture and making your way through the mountains of mysteries. You can follow the bread crumbs, the legends from locals—however small they may be—simply because they matter to you. You can trace the lines and connect the dots, however sparse they are. Though much has been lost, you will find much to love. Though not all can be reclaimed, much remains.

We ache on, always pining for home, carrying loss as a longing, a kind of homesickness for a home we all believe we are bound for.

> I want you to know that
> blood never belonged

in these brooks
and on this land.
I want you to know the
wind never set out
to carry the sound of
weeping in its whispers.
I want you to look to the
east and feel the earth rise
up to meet your tired feet.
I want you to look to the
west and see the sun dancing
a dance that looks
nothing like sorrow.
I want you to acknowledge
these hills, this home,
our hold on this holy land.
I want you to sing your song
to the Great Spirit—
of gratitude, of thanks,
of the dawn lighting
land with grace.

———

When the sun
sets, leave zinnias
at your doorstep,

tied with blossoms
from that bush in
your backyard.

———

Camellia, she is called,
in summer, staying
in winter, waiting
always here, always home,
always loving, always loving.

I saw an empty bird's nest
in the branch of a
camellia bush. Birds
that flew away from home.

Remember

- There is a grief that comes when you lose your home.
- Grief is a shadow stitched to story.
- Home is a holding place.
- You are everything you know you are.

Reflect

- Engage your senses and ponder memories of your
  first home. What color were the walls? What was the
  landscape outside the windows? What spices filled the
  kitchen? Where did you play, cry, and laugh?
- What do you know, or wish you knew, of your family's
  homeland or country of origin?
- Where is home to you? Is it a hometown or a country of
  birth? Why is it home to you?

Respire

- Inhale: Home is held.
- Exhale: In my heart.

Forget-me-not, *Myosotis*
Meaning: Forget me not

FORGET-ME-NOT
for Friendship

Kindred spirits are not so scarce as I used to think.

Anne Shirley (L. M. Montgomery,
Anne of Green Gables)[1]

I t's my thirteenth birthday and we walk like we are drunk, though we are not, from the corner gas station back to my house, staggering alongside Route 59. We swig vintage-style Coca-Cola and put candy cigarettes in our mouths, because we are teenagers in middle school and we think we know what cool looks like. At thirteen, these are the friends I carry closest, the ones forever etched into my heart. The chorus concerts, field days at school, running wild at recess. They know me and have known me, in and through the years, up to this very moment.

At thirteen, they are still my best friends, though I haven't seen them since I moved, about a year prior. And they are all here, all six of them, visiting me in my new home, miles away from where our friendships first began. They are the ones who know my crushes, and how they've changed. They are the ones who celebrated my birthday when it was the party at McDonald's, the party at Pizza Hut, and now they've come to sleep over and spend the night talking about boys and bad grades.

They sing "Happy Birthday" to me, give me a silver necklace with a softball charm, a token that whispers to me that I'm still a part of the team, still number 6 out there on the pitcher's mound—serving slow balls, the half windmill that arches over home plate and drops so unexpectedly that batters swing and miss. I'm still a part of the team, still one of them just like I've always been—joking around in our jerseys after games, fast-walking to catch the late bus before it pulls out of the school's parking lot.

They gather in my room, this thirteenth birthday, and it is like a promise to me that they won't forget me, that they won't fill my place. When the party's over and they leave, I save every one of our glass Coke bottles. I clean them out and keep them in my closet, as if holding on to them will also keep my friends close. We write letters to each other, keeping in touch, keeping kindled the flames of our friendship.

I pour my heart out, page after page, tuck careful confessions into envelopes and slip them into the mail. At first return letters come, but in time they are less and less, until they cease altogether. I'm no longer hearing about boys and bad grades. I no longer know who cut their hair or who got cut from sports or spring musicals. I'm no longer hearing about strict teachers, or nice teachers, or fun teachers. My mailbox grows empty while my heart grows cold. This first fracturing of my friendships, a crack that splits so bad it causes a canyon of a chasm, seems to be my rite of passage into adolescence. A lonely fourteenth birthday.

What memories do you have of childhood birthdays?

We all need those friends who welcome us to heave our whole selves, bringing all of who we are—every intricate insecurity and flaw. Without them we are misguided ghosts, going about our way waiting for someone to find us, to really find us, in the depths of all of who we are. To see us and to say the things we need to hear. That **we are wanted for who we are**, wanted for how we are.

> Sacred circles
> are safe; you'll
> feel it in your
> chest, your breath *breathing*
> unburdened.

Friendship matters because it matters to be seen, matters to invite another into the deepest wells of our hearts, just as they invite us into the deepest wells within their hearts. We bare our very souls, confessing the things we've seen and thought, our dreams and deepest fears. And losing a friendship matters too, because it is like losing a part of ourselves, forever reminded that there is someone out there who knows us, who holds pieces of information about us, pieces *of* us.

The loss is great because the love is great. It's completely tragic for someone to enter into our story only to lose them all at once. We don't know how to function in the world anymore. We lose these people who gave us a place, gave us space to feel safe, to be all of who we are. We lose friends in so many different ways. Sometimes through moving, sometimes through new jobs. Sometimes through distance, sometimes through disagreements. We lose them when we're young and we lose them as adults. We lose them for reasons clear as day and we lose some through mysteries that remain.

What's unique and jarring about this loss is that compared to death, which may be "a body without a goodbye," losing a friendship is a "goodbye without a body."[2] It is an ending without clear closure—not a funeral, not a last look, not a hug, not even a handshake. It's another ambiguous loss; there is no finality, no person on the other end to tidy things up before the parting takes place.

Friendship losses are a lot like fissures, a cracking in the middle of a cliff, causing a separation though both hearts are still beating. It is hard to reconcile that someone we used to know lives apart from knowing us—is alive and well, seemingly, without us.

In this, we also lose the ability to trust, to open ourselves and to be vulnerable, to bear our hearts and risk it all again. In all my living, I can't recall places that have given time for processing the dissipation of friendships. In all my moving, I don't recall conversations to make space for these earth-shattering, not-so-little losses.

This is when and why I became a pen pal, a writer of letters. I sought so desperately to cling to the ones I loved. Writing letters, holding the line on our connections. I didn't want to let go. I didn't know how to.

> Find me a friend
> I can keep till the end
>
> Find me a friend who
> will help me to mend
>
> Find me a friend
> I can give to without end
>
> Find me a friend
> To them I will send
>
> All.

The first time I had the faintest example of the beautiful depth and sincerity that a friendship could hold was when I watched *Anne of Green Gables*, a movie based on the 1908 novel by L. M. Montgomery. I snuck the VHS from my mother's stack of movies and watched, over and over, the story of this orphan girl as she arrives at the train station, carpetbag in hand, and heads to Green Gables, the place that eventually becomes her forever home. Anne, an orphan with no family and no friends, creates an imaginary friend in the reflection from a bookcase with glass doors. Anne tells her new guardian, Marilla:

I used to pretend that my reflection in it was another little girl who lived in it. I called her Katie Maurice, and we were very intimate. I used to talk to her by the hour, especially on Sunday, and tell her everything. Katie was the comfort and consolation of my life. We used to pretend that the bookcase was enchanted and that if I only knew the spell I could open the door and step right into the room where Katie Maurice lived, instead of into Mrs. Thomas' shelves of preserves and china. And then Katie Maurice would have taken me by the hand and led me out into a wonderful place, all flowers and sunshine and fairies, and we would have lived there happy for ever after.[3]

Anne, accustomed to loneliness and living without family or friends, resorts to creating her own friend—a perfect one at that—in her imagination. Katie Maurice is everything Anne needs her to be—everything, perhaps, that Anne wants to be. She is accessible, quick to forgive, and confined to Anne's imagination, subject to her will and wants. She doesn't talk back, nor does she talk about Anne. Katie Maurice is unlike those who have failed Anne before; Anne never has to worry about losing her or being disappointed by her.

Then comes Diana Barry, a girl Anne becomes acquainted with at Green Gables. The two find each other when they're most in need—Anne with her head in the clouds and Diana with her nose in her books. As the series folds in and out of Anne's life, it turns out Anne doesn't just make friends for herself. Unwittingly, she teaches others about friendship, the importance of imaginative hope, and seeing the good in others.

The two girls get into their fistful of contentions, but all is fair in love and war. They fight, they make up, and they strengthen the bonds of their friendship, following each other throughout their individual life journeys filled with marriage and studies and children. The beauty and power in Anne's story is not merely that she makes a friend but *how* she makes a friend. To become the kindred spirits that she and Diana become, Anne has to get outside of her head. She has to leave her imagination and enter the realm of mortals, of humans with the propensity to mishandle her trust and break her heart. To befriend Diana Barry is the most vulnerable thing Anne can do, putting herself in the path of loss, all for the sake of friendship.

Who was your imaginary friend?

I wrote these words in *Let There Be Art* that still echo deep within, as if they were embedded into my bones, reverberating along the length of my body. Reeling in my own reality, another season of fractured friendships and learning the lesson that loss invades even this too, I wrote:

> We lose friends just as soon as we learn to love them. We move and we make new ones. We are broken by them and we break them ourselves.[4]

It is another inevitable loss that looms large around life's corners of change, coming in with the seasons, with and without reason. A friend falls out of our inner circle; we begin to notice the relationship is suspended in a sort of ambivalence.[5] Schedules change, geography drives division. There is truth to that and space for the separation. There is permission for the process and grace for needing to grieve the journey. But there isn't one of us, not a soul, who could sit sane on this spinning world without a friend to call our own, real or imaginary. It is as Karen Swallow Prior argues in *On Reading Well*: "We need companionship," she writes. "So badly that if we lack it, we will create the illusion of it."[6]

Friends offer the secret and sacred holding of every unsung sorrow, every lingering fear, the hell we've seen and the glory we've glimpsed. Still, while loss may very well be part of your life, it doesn't have to be a legacy. Loss doesn't have to be the thing that defines you in your death—that you were too afraid to love, or too afraid to lose, or both, and that you chose instead to live alone.

To befriend another is to believe in the miracle of hope after heartache. It's to willingly split the heart open for the possibility of being chosen. That young girl I was, the one who felt the crack that caused a canyon of a chasm? She found new friends, and then new friends again. She split her heart open, walked through the front doors of homes, sat on crumb-covered couches and the creaky porch swings of friends that live just down the road and to the right.

You and I can do just as Anne Shirley does when it comes to knowing and believing that "Kindred spirits are not so scarce as [she] used to think."[7] While the world burns with people who will break your heart and betray you, or lie and leave you lonely, it also waxes with wonderful souls—seeds waiting to take root and blossom in your life.

> *Who are the friends you carry in your sacred circle?*

You are not alone in the world, not a face looking into shards of the mirror, talking back to your reflection and believing in something that is not really there. Release yourself from your haunted histories, from the grip of those who left you grieving though they still walk this earth, roaming wild and free. See beyond the brokenness of others and of yourself; believe there is a soul, or two, or three, that can soothe instead of sting. They will befriend you because they will see you, the real you.

You'll see that you are wanted for who you are.

Wanted for how you are.

> Flowers for you,
> Forget-me-nots,
> hand-delivered,   *so smothered in my hands*
> they withered.

———

I promise I won't forget you, not
the way your wrinkles smiled
when you laughed, all that radiant sun,
or the color of your hair,
the shape of your eyebrows framing your
still-compassionate eyes.
We are separated by miles, now,
chasing pavements and
crossing chasms in our sleep—
the lies we tell ourselves
when we're awake.
I carry you, still, in the center of my chest,
now caving in after all these years
of shallow breath,
lungs limping, free
at the very
memory of you.

———

Kindred is a
kind of kiss
that dares keep
kindness from
going amiss.

———

For the furry friends
we've lost along the way—
the ones who held our worlds
when no one else would.
There is a place for you,
here, in the midst of these
words that reach to enfold.
You were the first of friends,
the faithful friends,

the following friends,
the unforgetting friends.
And here is where
your name
belongs.

Remember

- We are wanted for who we are.
- Friendship matters because it matters to be seen.
- The loss is great because the love is great.
- To befriend another is to believe in the miracle of hope after heartache.

Reflect

- What memories do you have of childhood birthdays?
- Who was your imaginary friend?
- Who are the friends you carry in your sacred circle?

Respire

- Inhale: Friendships have fallen.
- Exhale: Friendships will flourish.

Edelweiss, *Leontopodium*
Meaning: Courage

EDELWEISS
for Dreams

My girl, some boats are made for the river and some for the
ocean. And there are some that can go anywhere because
they always know the way home.

Granny June (Angeline Boulley, *Firekeeper's Daughter*)[1]

I take the bus down to the city, get off at Port Authority near
Columbus Circle, and get myself to the Hearst Tower, off 57th
Street and Eighth Avenue in Midtown Manhattan.

I walk through the tall glass doors, looking up to see a cascade of
water dancing down the sides of the staircase. I take the escalator
and ascend to where light ricochets from the windows as the sun
shines through, smiling over Central Park and cityscape. I sit down
for my interview with *Seventeen* magazine, talk about how I love to
write and how I'm interning with a publisher right now and how
I can catch on quickly. I talk about my love of the magazine and
all the many reasons for which I'd be the perfect person to intern
with their team.

I see my future spanning before me: a hotshot editor, living and
working in the city of my dreams, the city where both of my parents

have worked and found their identity and purpose. I lose myself in thought, find myself in the myriad of made-up moments playing out before me. I can and will make it happen, the life that was and will always be meant for me.

The editors at *Seventeen* invite me to stay in touch, to reach back out for the next semester. I hop on some city bus, take it all the way back up over the bridge, and let the dreams lie dormant in my head and heart until the next year when it comes time to reach out and return. Because the dream was always to "make it" and move there. Get a job, get rich, and survive the city—subway system and all.

Now I just needed to make it work. All that was left was to find an apartment and get a job to carry me through while interning. I make plans to spend a few weeks at home after graduation, to rest a little before making it all come together.

Then June comes like an unsuspected thief. I've only been home for two weeks or so when my older brother's nanny of four years quits. Hands in her letter, says that it is time. My chest tightens, and questions come spilling in. *What will this mean for my mother? What will this mean for my brother?* And, more importantly, *What will this mean for me?* I consider how this might be my life, my dreams on the line. I feel my heart spin and turn within me. The fast-slow breaths of my chest rising and falling.

I know how the scenario will pan out. Late-night searching online for nannies. The interviews and questions. The face scanning and the background checks. Like blind speed dating—all the effort poured into seeing who would be safe enough to take care of my older brother. To be his nanny, his keeper.

"I'll do it," I utter. My brain barely has the chance to unfold and recognize what I've just said. "I can take care of him. I can be his nanny."

I watch my dream wash down the gutter, like strong currents of sidewalk rain in New York City come rushing in, sinking it fast and down and hard.

What was the first dream you ever had for your life?

Dreams die, fold up, and altogether fall out of the sky. They are ripped right from our rib cage, taken from the hollow of our hand. **We lose dreams and we lay them down.** And I want to know if—without a shadow of doubt—there is honor in laying down our dreams for the sake of our loved ones. I want to know if there can be any good in walking away from a dream. I want to know what becomes of the path paved before us as we make decisions in regard to our dreams. Is it all haphazard, or will it all work out anyway? No matter which way the coins are tossed, no matter which choice is made.

Your words have the power to name the dreams that mattered.

Dreams die, but dreams matter. How do we reconcile the two, then? Make sense of our lives, our pain, our purpose? How do we look out over the expanse of our life, admit the dreams that have died, and still have hope enough to dream again? How do we unearth purpose when the path before us is painted over with pain?

Dreams matter,
the world tells you.

Dreams die,
your life hands you.

On silver-plated platters, life delivers dreams and then demands we lay them down to rest. When the kids fall ill, when finances fail, when bodies betray, when jobs derail. More than sympathetic sayings, we need space to grieve these lost dreams—every big one and little one and those in between. We need room to rage about the ruin, places we can place our pain.

You need a truth to tell yourself when you're lost in the fog, hope for the hours when purpose evades and the point of life eludes you. Your words have the power to name the dreams that mattered. For **a dream is the dwelling place of a deep desire.** And this desire came from somewhere, came from a place that was cultivated deep down.

> Attend to the desire,
> even if the dream has died.

> The dream is but a house,
> a *how* for *what*
> you can't live
> without.

Dig up the deep, dark earth. Lay the dream to rest, and let tears fall as you do. While you're there, excavate the grounds of your dreams for the seeds that once held them. Look for the longing, which will long outlive the dream. Tell yourself again that it matters for your becoming and your being in the world.

> What if dreams are
> like diamonds
> in the dirt,

> waiting to be mined
> *and* refined?

It wasn't a ravenous fire that killed my dreams; it was a slow burn, a smoldering until it was too late to save what remained. That is how it is when dreams die—they're smothered slowly. They fill up the air with a thick, dense fog that haunts like some cruel reminder.

As you think about lost dreams, what emotions, images, or feelings come to mind?

There is one character who would understand the haunting of dreams lost full well. In Angeline Boulley's debut novel, *Firekeeper's Daughter*, Daunis Fontaine is an eighteen-year-old half-Native, half-white unenrolled tribal member. She first loses her uncle while trying to figure out her plans for college. Burdened by this grief, her grandmother suffers from a stroke, all of which leads Daunis to forgo leaving for college to study medicine. In an attempt to spare her family from enduring a third bad thing, a literal tribal superstition that *bad things happen in threes*, she defers her dream and stays home for the sake of remaining close to her family.

> Eighteen years ago, my arrival changed my mother's world. Ruined the life her parents had preordained for her. I am all she has left in this world.
> Gramma Pearl always told me, *Bad things happen in threes.*
> Uncle David died in April.
> GrandMary had a stroke in June.
> If I stay home, I can stop the third bad thing from happening.
> Even if it means waiting a little longer to follow the Plan.[2]

So Daunis stays, lays down her longing, pushes her passion to the side, and lets her dream die. Her journey is filled with disappointment, pain, rage, and grief. But it is also filled with self-discovery, courage, revelation, and redemption. In the smallest, unassuming way, she is presented with the opportunity to use her passion for medicine, the desire that drives her dreams, and in that she is fulfilled. Faced with the choice to be a part of something bigger than herself, she embarks upon an adventure filled with thrilling suspense and intergenerational trauma within her tribe—a journey that changes not only her life but the lives of all those she knows. Eventually, at the end of the book, she finally does set out to follow her dream of studying medicine in college.

At this part of her journey, the dream is no longer simply about her intelligence or her striving for success. Instead, she has come face-to-face with grief interwoven with goodness. She stares at them both, touched and equally changed by them. She knows what she wants not only for herself but for the people she loves. Her dream becomes more than just her shot at success; it becomes a medium through which to serve her people.

Even still, while this is all noble, it is also very nuanced. So often a journey is passed over with platitudes. How can we begin to honor the heartache that comes when change charts a new path, when trauma interrupts the trajectory of our lives, when loss is layered over our longings?

How can you honor the heartache that came when change charted a new path in your life?

The path filled with dead dreams is painful because it preys upon purpose. In the quiet of the night, the shadow of dead dreams whispers into thin air to enchant us to wonder, seriously ponder, if there is anything worthwhile about life. It is paved with pain because it steals a part of us, takes from that which has called out to us, cultivated compassion within us, chiseled us.

I want to whisper a word to you, want you to "roll the word around on your tongue for a bit," as Donald Miller once wrote.[3]

Desire.

We can look to the desire that lies deep beneath the dream. We can welcome redirection—by way of loss, by way of laying down. Why? Because, at the core, it is the desire we intend to live for and from. Tell me—as you wonder what could have been, have you ever stopped to think about the beauty of what became?

In giving up my dream to go away for my undergraduate studies (before my dream of working in New York City), I stayed closer to home, closer to my family, and enrolled in a local college. On December 13, 2019, I shared on Instagram a reflection on this redirection:

I studied writing in the same small town where my grandfather was killed, walked the holy halls of a college covered in colorful prayers echoing throughout its acres. When I first enrolled, I thought I'd be a missionary teacher. I had dreams of living over the seas, knee deep in a culture that was not mine, with a people that was not mine, loving them with a love that was not mine. But the dream died at an awakening of the realization that my heart wasn't cut out for a classroom. So I returned home that first summer with the label "Undeclared" seared into my bones. The undeclared degree was, deep down, an undeclared dream. And, that summer, I returned home and ran to my writing. Sprawled out on my bed, writing songs with the keyboard I slept with and an untuned guitar. In the dark of my room, flames on candles burning, and my pen raging between thin lines on thick pages. Words swelled within, like a call, like a voice calling out my name. The only peace I ever felt was when I answered that call, brought my burning self like a boat to a beckoning sea. After I signed my life away in the financial aid office, everyone asked what I would do with a degree in writing. Photojournalism, I told them. Work at Random House, I told them. Write books and songs, I told them. I don't know, I told them. Move the world like a missionary, I should have told them. Love long on people across wide spaces, I should have told them. Unfold beauty and grief in syncopated measure, I should have told them. Gather souls, weary and broken, to tend to until a mending makes way deep into the heart, I should have told them.[4]

I stayed.

I retracted my bird wings and circled the nest home. I stayed. I found that staying meant acquiring more memories of my older brother, memories I can recall now without much thought. The memory I cradle now is of me watching him as he begins to seize. There, his rattling rib cage looks to be choking his lungs. He seizes so long his face turns red. Now purple. Now blue.

His eyes roll back, all while he is hitting his head against the floor—my twenty-four-year-old big brother. And his hands—the fingers are curled and cramped up. There is spit foaming, and the spit hits my face. I cradle him on the floor, body rolled over, seemingly lifeless. Rip open the diaper and spread the cheeks. Lungs heaving, my fingers fumble to find the hole needed to make this injection. I push Valium in, slowly, until the syringe stops with a click. This is the very thing I wanted to escape. The very thing I wanted to get away from. The very thing going far away for college would have kept me from.

That day, for the first time, in all the many diapers I'd changed and all the drool I'd wiped from his face, I saw a tear. One solitary tear, falling from his eye while turned on his side. And I swear, in that moment I saw right through his eyes and inside his body, where there was not only a broken brain but also a broken heart, hurting, tired, afraid, and alone.

I didn't just see a body broken and in need of fixing.

I saw my older brother hurting and in need of love.

Did God need to break something in me? Break my heart wide open to the reality that I was filled with a confusion devoid of any compassion? Was he trying to show me that it didn't matter how much I wished the hardship away if I couldn't actually sit in my older brother's heartache?

Have you ever "sat" in someone else's heartache? What was their heartache and what did it feel like?

After college, I stayed home and gave up my dream of publishing books to change the diapers of a full-grown man, a blow that stings and hollows a hole in me still. But then I see his smile radiant in the reflection of bubbles, hear him laugh, and it tells me his brain knows freedom even though his caged body doesn't, and that brightens me up more than any light reflecting off city skyscrapers ever could.

Grieve what you gave up, let the tears fall. Know, in all of your longing and living, that you are not here to be a hero—you are a human. You are not here to save lives but to serve them. Carry this truth as you live out your days, leaving jobs jaded and deferring dreams for whatever reasons you know you must. You are a boat that can go anywhere, no matter which way the wind blows or howls. No matter the detours, or dreams dead or deferred, let your desire to serve be what leads you on.

> Edelweiss, *yes,*
> for the everyday
> courage to endure
> the climb, of ladders
> leaning against
> tall towers
> with glass
> ceilings. Edelweiss,
> *for broken dreams,*
> for courage: to
> dare, and dream,
> and do, again.

> ———

> The dream died
> and it didn't come
> back for me.
>
> Do I stay or
> do I go? Do I
> wait? How do
> I go
>
> from here?

> ———

89

I dare you to dig
deeper than you ever have before,
down beneath the layers
that you know by heart.
Dig deeper, reaching to your soul.
Hear those sacred whispers
tell you where, and how, to go.

Remember

- We lose dreams and we lay them down.
- A dream is the dwelling place of a deep desire.
- Grieve what you gave up.

Reflect

- What was the first dream you ever had for your life?
- As you think about lost dreams, what emotions, images, or feelings come to mind?
- How can you honor the heartache that came when change charted a new path in your life?
- Have you ever "sat" in someone else's heartache? What was their heartache and what did it feel like?

Respire

- Inhale: My dreams are deep.
- Exhale: My desires are deeper.

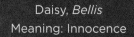

Daisy, *Bellis*
Meaning: Innocence

DAISY

for Innocence

The world has taken away too much from you to still be
considered a child.

M'Baku (*Black Panther: Wakanda Forever*)[1]

I wear white on this one day, because that is what the world
tells you to do when your heart is ready to stand before rows
of souls and whisper a lifetime of vows that will slip into thin
air the second they leave sacred lips.

Sheer white curtains blow in the wind at a park, outside in Montgomery, New York. My arm interlocked, tethered to the tailored suit
of a man towering over my frame, his Black hands now releasing
me. I see a vision through my veil, a blur of faces I cannot decipher
because I am barely breathing, seeing stars from the corset wrapped
tight around my chest, all the while looking to the one I am there
to pledge my life away to.

I echo the words prepared for me, seal them into the wind of witnesses watching this matrimony, and we kiss. I do not remember the
sight or sound of these few seconds, but candid moments captured
in still shots tell me I smile with joy the whole way through, my
bouquet of coral roses and blue thistle held high in the air.

Minutes later, I am behind the bathroom with my bare body. My mother is there, in a fuchsia dress that brings out the brightness of her beautiful face, and my mother-in-law is gracious in her hanbok, the same kind of gown I will soon be wearing. Together, the three of us whisk off my wedding dress, and they hold me, tenderly, while I sink my frame into Korea's silk tradition, rich in ancient stories, histories I know not of.

And the whole day is a celebration, but it is also sad because it's a sort of leaving, my last chance to say "goodbye to all that."[2] Isn't it true that new love welcomes new loss? So I smile in front of the camera, but I sob deeply into the shoulders of the ones I hug, and there is a pit in the depth of my stomach, the kind of knowing that flashes with a certainty that *this is it*—this is the end of the life I once knew. You can only merge so many worlds together before they fracture, before they fall in and out of another. One must fade and fall away while you attend to the other.

> Pieces fragment,
> time evades.
> Little losses leaking,
> *drip, drip, drip.*

I say goodbye to my parents and leave my room, the four coffee-colored walls that hold my secrets, and I leave my school and my friends and Elsie's Luncheonette, my favorite corner café in which to eat blueberry pancakes and watch police officers eating their breakfast on break. I leave family gravesites behind, never again to brush my hands along gravestones on their wanting grounds. I leave the roads I know by heart, leave the faces who have seen me grow.

I marry, only to fall into the bed and body of a man whom I greet with my grief, entangled with love. I wed and marry a man, leaving all behind to build a new life, and so maybe I am a little naive, a little uninformed about how this whole marriage thing works, how the bones of your past do not just get buried under the soil of a new start.

Where is the manual on marriage, where is the scroll of sacred secrets telling us how this covenantal gift is also a goodbye that brings grief? And where are the warnings in the wind telling you how questions will come in the quiet of night, giving you away to flashbacks and fears, waking you to wrestle and wonder whether you should have worn a white dress or not? Because memories will unwrap moments you've long tried to forget, flashbacks of unwelcome hands in unholy ways—marring the mind, scarring the body until it keeps score—tallies that tell of the times when life took and never gave back.

What is the story your flashbacks tell you? Do they tell tales of the times when life took and never gave back?

There is a word for the ones who lose by way of wounds brought on by human hands, even when it's a hidden harm, a burden held beneath the bones in secret and silence, such as my own. It can be carried for years, some for decades, forgotten far under the floorboards of a beating heart. Dr. Clarissa Estés writes of a word that, these days, is often used to describe a person of no knowing, a simpleton, and that this modern definition is slightly different from the original meaning, the very etymology, of the word.[3] I see it too, now that I know this. Having studied Latin and learned the way of separating words into their various parts—the roots from endings, prefixes and suffixes—I see it now when I look at the word.

Innocent.

When broken down, *innocent* deconstructs into two root parts— *in*, meaning "not," and *nocēns*, meaning "injuring, doing harm, hurting."[4] It is the smallest differentiation that makes the biggest difference because, truly, someone who is innocent is not merely someone who is without guilt; rather they are someone without the knowledge of harm. Moreover, an innocent is not only not guilty of evil nor merely unaware of evil in the world but rather is one who is without wound.

To lose one's innocence, then, is to lose the existence of a life that knows no pain. To lose one's innocence is to heave heavy, to breathe bruised, to wake in a world where you not only see hurt but *feel* it too. To lose one's innocence is to lose the wholeness of body, mind, and soul. It is to sustain pain—all of which, by the way, was never the plan.

Pain didn't come until after the fall. **Pain is the fruit that was never meant to come to fruition.** And now the innocent is all of us, each one of us holding hurt that should have never happened, pain we should have been protected from. All the things we wish we could unsee and unhear. Children displaced by the 2022 Russian invasion of Ukraine paint pictures of the "bloodied soldiers and buildings on fire" they saw.[5] Survivors of the September 11, 2001 attacks still hear "the sound of bodies being smashed to the ground."[6]

> Bodies encode the chaos,
> make memories of
> moments in need of
> mourning; a flash,
> like light from
> the shutter of a lens,
> captures trauma
> trains the brain
> *triggertriggertrigger.*

Do we talk about it enough? Do we talk about it enough in families, with friends gathered in circles by firesides, in churches? Do we talk about the wounds and the wreckage, or ways through them? And if we do, what do we say to the one in six American women who have been victims of rape, the ones whose worlds are forever turned black?[7] What do we do for the millions of Ukrainian children in crisis?[8] What about the Katrina Babies like Cierra Chenier, stepping out of shadows of silence and telling her story, talking about how "all innocence was lost" at the realization that her home was gone, forever heartbroken by how "six feet of water took away my childhood."[9]

> *What stories hold the loss of your innocence? What people or places painted your world black? What choices led to the wounds you now walk with?*

It begins with a prayer.

Shuri, younger sister of King T'Challa, the Black Panther, prays, a plea to the god of her Wakandan people. She is desperate, in need of some kind of miracle, for she is trying, through technology, to save her brother, who is quickly dying. Shuri's miracle doesn't come soon enough, though, for T'Challa dies. And Shuri, along with all of Wakanda, is thrust into a paradigm of pain.

They proceed with a processional, adorned in the finest white garments, filled with song and weeping—a Wakandan ritual. And all the while this grief on the screen is real and felt. Layers deep, the characters in mourning are also the cast in mourning, all grieving the same and shared loss of Chadwick Boseman, the beloved actor who played Black Panther in the movie of the same name. And we, the audience, feel and know this loss too. As we reel in the climate of a pandemic world in the thick of racial tensions, we mourn with the characters and cast, grieving Wakanda's king and protector, the Black Panther.

Of *Black Panther: Wakanda Forever*, *Forbes* contributing writer Mark Hughes says:

> This is a story of a family and a people who must confront a terrible loss, only to be overwhelmed by events heaping greater loss upon them, testing their strength to the breaking point and beyond. They grieve for their King, for their hero and their inspiration, and for their shattered sense of invincibility. Everything seemed possible, and now everything feels lost.[10]

Black Panther: Wakanda Forever is stacked up with little loss upon little loss, and it is embedded with a grief that is great. And yet while this story is one of shared grief, truly it is Shuri who bears the brunt of it all. "If I sit and think about my brother for too long," she laments, "it won't be these clothes I burn. It will be the world."[11] The clothes she is referring to are the funeral garments she wore to her brother's burial, for it is a Wakandan ritual to burn them as an act of coming out of a period of mourning.

However, consumed with grief and rage, Shuri first refuses to participate in this ritual. Her mourning is not over; it still burns full and strong and deep. In typical Marvel Cinematic Universe fashion, as the movie wages on, so does war. In this, Shuri now also tragically loses her mother and, as the sole survivor of her family, is reluctantly thrust into a position of political power. Wakanda needs protection in the middle of its costly war with the nation of Talokan, an underwater kingdom in the Atlantic Ocean.

Swiftly, entirely, Shuri loses all and gains everything. The weight of global grief is placed on her shoulders; meanwhile, she is but a child, a college-aged kid thriving in her technological pursuits and passion. I am struck by this, by the complexity of Shuri's circumstances, the realities and roles that both break and take from her.

In two different instances, Shuri is shown clothed in her fine white funeral garments. The first time she grieves is at her brother's burial. The second time is for her mother. She is torn and unable to separate personal rage from her position of rule; her cousin, M'Baku, approaches to ask Shuri for her counsel on a decision regarding the safety of the Wakandan people. "So, now you are keen to hear from a child," Shuri responds bitterly. Then M'Baku, whose character often satisfies the role of comic relief, delivers one of the most powerful lines in the movie. To Shuri, he says: "The world has taken away too much from you to still be considered a child."[12]

The world has taken, the world has touched, the world has turned your eyes to see more than you should. It has trained you to know more than you should, do more than you should; you've tallied loss after loss and it hurts, incurable wounds gaping wide and lonely and real and raw.

It crushes
|
because it was
|
never meant
|
to be carried
||||||||||||||||||||||||
by you.

What weight(s) has the world placed on you?

The world will have you believe that there is no space to spare in bearing your burdens, in grieving your losses, namely that of your innocence. It will beg of you to comply, cover up your wounds, come and conform to what is normal and what is needed. Esteeming reputation and fearing retribution, the world will shame you into silence, carving out corners to keep you quiet and contained.

Your takers, or abusers, or leaders, or rulers, will purport that, because it happened forever and a day ago, it does not matter. That by now you should have magically, mysteriously mended. They will say that because the fragments are fuzzy they must be fiction. The world will tell you that silence saves and shame is a song. Its laws cannot, will not, label your "little" loss, which is not large enough to lead to legal action. Your loss is unwarranted because it went unwitnessed, and it will reduce you to testimony and trials. The world will tell you that if there is such a hurt it can heal, and there is hope, and the searing pain will someday become a scar, a story worth telling others.

You must know, and I fear perhaps you already do know, that the world cannot stitch up that gaping hole from which memory spills, cannot erase the images that come flashing like fireworks frightening the black sky of night. The world will not wake in the middle of the night to stop the story from asserting itself. There is this one thing, though, a tool to use to reconcile with all that is lost and lies in ruin.

Ritual.

We can find hope and help through ritual. Like Shuri, who eventually embraces the traditions of her people and learns how to mourn and hold sacred space for searing loss, we can reclaim ritual. Like Shuri, who eventually emerges from grief to burn her white funeral garments, we too can find grace to grieve and climb toward comfort. We are not characters in a movie counting losses. We are hurting humans, and our pain is not only perceived but palpable. And for this we need tangible ways in which **we can be present with our pain**, not merely try to make it pass through.

Amy Davis Abdallah, professor of theology and author of *The Book of Womanhood*, writes of a simple grief ritual she's come to claim. "I've started lighting a candle every time I lose something," she writes. "I light a candle when I face the kind of loss that causes grief—from the seemingly insignificant grief of the loss of time with friends during a pandemic year, to the more recognizable grief of death—I light a candle."[13]

She's noting something many of us can easily do but often do not realize. We can honor the small things with even the smallest rituals of remembrance. We can carve a sacred holding into our most mundane moments. **We can light candles for little losses**, for all the hidden harms we hold in our hearts.

When memories come flooding, we can light wicks and watch flickering flames, bring ourselves to stillness as we attend to our pain. The lighting of a candle is a metaphor, an image telling us the truth of our time here on this earth. It is brief, but it is beautiful. It *burns*, but

it
is
beautiful.

The loss of innocence is in little moments too.

It is in the moments when you receive a diagnosis and come face-to-face with the inevitability of mortality. It is sometimes in the choices we make that lead to the consequences we wade and walk through. It is when a child sees their first dead insect—like my son, frozen in disbelief at the look of lifelessness. We've created a ritual, he and I, a tangible way to memorialize the moment and move through the shock and sorrow. Whenever we see dead caterpillars, ants, rhinoceros beetles, or dragonflies, we cover them with leaves. It's as if we are shielding them from further harm, giving witness to what was and saying *We see you.*

> Small sacraments
> make meaning out
> of mystery, make
> space for making
> sense of sorrow.

We wax with wounds as the years go by, losing more and more to brokenness. The world takes and takes and takes. We lose things and things are lost to us. We break and are burdened; we see and hear the one thousand earthquakes that we'll never unsee, never unhear. We've lost our unknowingness. We know too much to be innocent. Some of these moments bring about positive realities. Some bring devastation. Someone dies. A child moves and loses touch with friends. They experience for the first time a glimpse, if not all, of what adults know and experience to be true: nothing lasts forever, the world is filled with pain and unfulfilled promises, wars are waged, pestilence is prevalent, and not everyone is safe or can be trusted.

The white world is colored red, colored in all the hues that make us vulnerable to seeing the world as it really is. We are not mere children covering and shielding our eyes. We go to sleep and wake to the reality that the world has changed—that *we've* changed too.

Indeed, *we sit down to dinner, and life as we know it changes.*[14]

Might our hearts
burn bright and burn warm
never grow cold.
Though the world
takes and takes and takes
might we still
give and give and give—

from love and *for* love.

—————

They say it's a weed,
a *common* wee**d**.
A pest to be pulled
from the gr**a**ss and ground.
But I think it's kind of resilient,
this common weed with white petals,
its purity **i**n plain sight.
And I find it kind of ironic, that
thi**s** thing they call a common weed
has a name and colors our world
in defiant shades and shapes of jo**y**.

—————

I am looking for just one
word—in foreign faces,
in the hollow of a hand,
in unspoken spaces, in
the many moments
of looking into
familiar eyes.

Just one
along the way that
will speak of spots
and stains, or broken brains,
or time-lost trains.

Just one word,
in the face of a stranger
to tell me
all is not lost.

All is not lost.

Remember

- Pain is the fruit that was never meant to come to fruition.
- We can find hope and help through ritual.
- We can be present with our pain.
- We can light candles for little losses.

Reflect

- What is the story your flashbacks tell you? Do they tell stories of the times when life took and never gave back?
- What stories hold the loss of your innocence? What people or places painted your world black? What choices led to the wounds you now walk with?
- What weight(s) has the world placed on you?

Respire

- Inhale: The world is dark.
- Exhale: I light a candle.

Chamomile, *Matricaria*
Meaning: Energy in adversity

CHAMOMILE

for Calm

Thank you for saving me.

Tony Stark (*Iron Man*)[1]

First I marry the man I love. We live in love for six short months. Then, he goes from beholding my body to bathing it in a porcelain tub. My legs are weak; he runs water, and it feels like a shiver on my skin.

I sit there hunched over, muscles twitching and weighed with a bone-tired kind of heaviness I've never felt before. *Compassion.* I feel it through my husband's hands. But he is also just as confused as I am, and in his eyes I see something that looks like fear. We do not know what is happening, and we do not have money or insurance to figure it out. We are out of pennies, out of promises, and suddenly the whole world is spinning—a kaleidoscope of colors, enrapturing what is unknown and uncertain, in all shapes and sizes.

Where is the world when you need someone to hold your hand because the walls are spinning and your heart is beating like a powwow drum? Where is God when the white coats are tying tourniquets like bows on your arm, tapping for veins to take blood and give fluids? Where is God when you've altogether lost it—lost feeling in your fingers and lost faith?

What do you say when you're the one in the hospital gown, standing on cold floors with bare feet? What do you say when the tests come back negative, nothing to show, and now they really want to know if it's possible that you're pregnant, or maybe there's some drug you've taken that you're not telling them about?

I fumble over my words, tell them I am being honest, that I don't know what could be causing my body to crumble. They don't hear me, though. Either that or they don't want to. Tell me:

> If a body breaks
> in the light of day, and
>
> *n o o n e*
>
> is around to hear it,
> does it make a sound?

I can tell you what it's like to be a twenty-six years old and unsure of your body's urge to use the bathroom. Maybe you know it too? What it's like to feel your husband's hands wrapping around your waist, not to pull you in for a slow kiss but because your legs are not moving, are not getting the message from your brain to step, to walk.

Maybe you know what it's like to stumble across a stone-cold hospital room while a friend walks your drip to the toilet and stands with you there, listening to you mumble incoherent apologies for everything that's spilling out of the not-so-better half of you.

My heart throbs, but they send me home. Tell me to rest and eat, tell me I really should follow up with the doctors printed on the packet of papers they give me, the papers that say I'd been admitted for a *headache.*

> My world crumbles
> and they call it a headache.

Better off calling it a
heartache.

That night, and every night for what feels like thousands more, I lie awake, eyes staring into the still ceiling, breath hyperventilating and my brain telling me that I will die. I lie awake, a prisoner to pain in my body—but what hurts more is the crushing weight of all I cannot control.

Have you ever walked through a sickness or symptoms that were not believed?

I will never stop writing about this because it's a reality that will never quit, never quite go away: "**We use our bodies for everything.**"[2] And when our bodies break and we can no longer do these things, can no longer make or work or run or dance, something within us dies.

When you are diagnosed with a disease, when mind-crippling progressions take memories away, you don't just lose health, you lose habits. When you lose health, you lose life. Slowly, surely.

You don't just lose muscle,
you lose memory.
You don't just lose ability,
you lose stability.

The loss of fitness, of function, is a secondary loss that comes at the news of disease and diagnosis.[3] A hand is not just a hand, it is that which holds the hands of the ones you love. It's the grip that gives you the ability to hammer nails and build your home. Your skin is not just skin, it is the blanket of your whole body, a blanket that stretches and moves with you as you carry children, as you stretch out arms into the sky and whisper prayers of gratitude, anushiik, into thin air.

When it comes to the body, there is also the loss of our longevity. There is, as fate would have it, the truth of this fact: our bodies break down not only because of disease but because of measured breath, because of time. We wax with wrinkles, wisdom, and wiry gray hair, our bodies aging and changing because they cannot forever stay.

Once, I scrolled past an Instagram post by *National Geographic* that pictured an older man holding his nose and lying in a galvanized tub filled with ice water. I took a screenshot of the post. Not because I wanted to remember to read the article but because I didn't want to forget such a piece existed. The graphic read: "Can we 'cure' aging? Scientists are racing to crack the code."[4]

Can we "cure" aging? I didn't know we were trying to cure aging. As if we should. We want to undo creation's curse, as if we could. We want to appear ageless and reflect radiance. We want to discount disability, forget anything fallen or fractured about us. We want to "clean up the molecular and biochemical wreckage at the root of so many health problems in old age" (I eventually did read the article) so that we can live longer, live stronger.[5]

> What will cure
> our dis·ease
> with disease?

We want the cure for aging not only because we want to keep on living but because we want to keep our lives. We want to keep all of who we are—our memories, our thoughts, our stories. But as we age, and as our bodies break down, do we lose all we've ever been? Or do we grow, not merely in size but in space, expanding our capacity to contain the many ways in which we see and experience the world? Do we grow from all of the layers wrapped over our memories, our minds?

In her book *The Irrational Season*, Madeleine L'Engle writes, "After all, I am not an isolated fifty-seven years old; I am every other age I have been, one, two, three, four, five, six, seven . . . all the way up to and occasionally beyond my present chronology."[6]

"I am large, I contain multitudes," writes Walt Whitman.[7] I wonder, do our aging and changing bodies make space for the many multitudes that we are? Do we lose these parts—the dreams, the damage, the love, the loss? Or do they change with us? Stay with us, layered with and within us, perhaps even leading us? How do we make space for these layers, these multitudes of ourselves? **It is through all our layers we see and experience the world** . . . though bodies break, though age atrophies the mind.

When it comes to aging, what feelings or thoughts come to mind?

I'll tell you about the first film Marvel Studios independently wrote, directed, filmed, and featured, which as of December 2022 has also been "immortalized" in the National Film Registry that honors movies that have—in all their fantasy and fiction—made history.[8]

On May 2, 2008, director Jon Favreau released *Iron Man*, which cast Robert Downey Jr. as the character who would ultimately capture the compassion that is within all of us. It is inventor and industrialist Tony Stark, a witty man on an unintended journey from selfishness to selflessness, who unwittingly becomes Iron Man. Kidnapped, betrayed, and exploited for his knowledge, he is held in captivity and forced to create a weapon of mass destruction.

In the midst of this wild turn of events, Stark is injured during the kidnappers' attack. He sustains near-fatal heart damage and survives only because of an innovative implant made by Dr. Ho Yinsen, his fellow captive. Throughout this movie, the Iron Man series, and eventually the entire canon of Marvel movies that include Iron Man, he rises and falls within a character arc uniquely his—a man on a seeming journey from heartless to heartwarming.

Stark—who, mind you, is already marked by grief with the long-ago loss of his parents—goes on to endure more loss on top of the sustained physical damage to his heart and "invisible" loss of his health.

Consistent with the nature of loss, his character ebbs and flows through various stages of acceptance of his new reality: he survives only because he is both man and machine. He is kept alive by a makeshift heart implant. It turns out, however, that Iron Man's heart is not merely made of metal. Stark comes to embody that which is paradoxically presented in his very name. His heart, though made with iron through and through, beats not coldly but with warmth and compassion for the ones he loves and the citizens he seeks to save.

As you think about your life and health, what of your suffering or story has cultivated compassion for others and strength within yourself?

Disease, disability, and the decline of health can distort your world and turn the air around you dark and cold. You and your body can change, altogether crumble and crash—all of your todays in constant collision with your yesterdays and against all your could-have-been tomorrows.

We cannot stop the world from colliding, cannot stop the explosions from shocking and striking, but there is this—tilting our chins and turning our eyes to see the Good Doctor. There is hoping, praying that he might meet us in that dark cave. That deeply, daily we might feel him put his hands on us and pull the shrapnel from our hurting hearts, letting them beat with whatever strength they have left.

I weep, too, at the *would be* of my broken body. Weep with you and for you, for the limp in your leg, the disease doctors can't peg. I mourn for every metastasized swell of cells, every meaning-making center embedded within the walls of your skin. I weep for the many ways the world and doctors have demeaned and discounted your diagnosis of depression, anxiety, or bipolar disorder. I weep for how the world spins a violent cycle of days within seasons, seasons within time, and the need to carry on through our work, our weeks, as though we are not shattered.

I weep for your heart, too, spun tenderly but ever so tightly in the one thousand protective layers you hoped would keep it safe, and for the way you've succumbed to believing in the barriers you've built. Believing that you are fine and strong enough, that the thought of forever living a life laced with this kind of loss, however small or insignificant, however convenient it may seem in the light of another's, does not sometimes, if not always, bring a pang.

Has no one told you, really whispered to you, that your ailment—whether it's agonizing or only an ache—was never meant to be yours, in any capacity of any kind, any size, at any point in any time? Have you named it, really named it, for yourself? Not merely your diagnosis on paper but the diagnosis of your heart. That you have lost *something*—a strength, a dream, a hope—all because your body has bent toward brokenness.

You can grieve, even if it's but a sigh, again and again, deeply, daily, as you reach for the bottle of pills that remind you of the pain you cannot prevent. **There is space for you**, though, in this world that requires perfection and rejects you if you're anything but. There is still love for you, even when your need is always needing, even when your flesh is always failing despite the one thousand times you pleaded, the one thousand times you've prayed for God to take it all away.

You are held, even when sorrow stays.

May you live not as someone who must bend toward healing in order to live with meaning but rather knowing you are held, even when sorrow stays. Know that your daily dance and strain for health and wholeness are reminiscent of the One whose heart bends and moves the same.

> May this here
> poem give place
> for the protest
> of your pain.

Might empathy
enfold you,
eternity embolden
you.

To tell the truth
about the loss you know
however little,
however untold.

I see it in my mind: there I am on that bed, in that one place where bodies go undetected. My memory of the hospital that day stings like a stain I can never wash away, my body lying there, the beeping machines, and the doctors telling me everything is okay when it is not. Nothing within or about my body or my mind is okay. I'm breaking, burning—along with every preconceived notion of safety and security. While in the bed, my vitals are captured by the machines measuring my heart rate and testing my blood levels, but never once am I monitored or measured for my grief. No tests are taken of my sorrow. The white coats walk in and out, see me, attend to me, and yet there is not a soul witnessing my breakdown.

**Your wish for
witness is not a
weakness.**

To be seen is
to be held.
To be held
is to be
whole.

These feelings are not us failing. The interruption to our life is significant and worthy of working through, processing the pain, and understanding why we feel an overarching sense of hurt and grief. These are the disenfranchised losses, those not acknowledged by others. We minimize these losses because they are survivable, livable, manageable. Still, this does not make them hurt or haunt us any less. We breathe on because bones still hold up our bodies; we carry on, calling these losses insignificant when really they are consequential.

Someday these small pains may lead you to serve through your suffering, to give even while much is being taken. Someday the wisdom of your years will spill into the hearts of the ones who walk behind you. You'll tell them of the One you met in the deep, dark cave, the One who put his hands on you, pulled the shrapnel from your hurting heart. May your words drip with gratitude and grace. May the brokenness within you give way to the birth of bright days, however they come for you—singing, shining, sighing.

Some years after my body broke, I conceived and carried the heartbeat of a child. A whole life inside of my body, this body that I believed could never be strong, would never carry anything but wreckage and ruin.

Weeks morphed into months, and I swelled in size and in love, until the day came when I was in that one room with white sheets. Nurses slipping in, slipping out, whispering to me that it would snow and the city would be covered in a blanket of white—a beautiful way to bring a baby into this broken world that will break him too.

> I hope the earth breaks open
> and brings you all the:
>
> Chamomile for tea.
> Chamomile you need.
>
> Chamomile for calm.
> Chamomile for cure.
>
> Chamomile for nerve.
> Chamomile for all
> you didn't deserve.

———

I hope you come
across small doses
of hope, like tiny pills
painted white and nearly
weightless but carrying
cures within their capsules . . .
if not for the here and now, then
hallelujah, for someday.

———

Here is how to hold your bones,
how not to leave the skin
you live in, how not to forsake
the flesh that fails, how not to
scorn the cells that kill.
Here is how to dig yourself out
from deepest, darkest grounds and graves:
You, the caged bird that you are,
will sing and sing and sing and sing.
A song, a knowing sound, that
calls your heart to hope.
You are not dead, *yet*.
Breath still beckons,
heart still beats.
Your feeble frame may give way
to pain, to pills, to cobblestone paths
too hard to stand upon.
Your hands, cold as they are,
will cup the curve of your body.
And you will hold, as he holds—
in hope of glory—
the bruised, beloved bones of your body.[9]

Remember

- We use our bodies for everything.
- It is through all our layers we see and experience the world.
- There is space for you.
- Your wish for witness is not a weakness.

Reflect

- Have you ever walked through a sickness or symptoms that were not believed?
- When it comes to aging, what feelings or thoughts come to mind?
- As you think about your life and health, what of your suffering or story has cultivated compassion for others and strength within yourself?

Respire

- Inhale: My body is broken.
- Exhale: My body is holy.

Carnation, *Dianthus caryophyllus*
Meaning: Mother's eternal love

CARNATION
for Vilomah

> That's what matters right there. Cloth seats matter. Seat
> heaters matter. Airbags matter. The three of us matter. It's
> the tribe that matters. Who cares what she thinks? You
> know what matters. This is what matters here.
>
> Sean (*Pieces of a Woman*)[1]

I see her in my mind, always. I remember the round of her face and the thin of her eyes. I see the gait of her walk, the glitch in her stride that, if only it could speak, might sound slurred. Her spine, slouched and slanted, bends as if she carries the weight of all life on her left side. And then her hand long-hanging, with the other placed upon her protruding belly, gently just so.

When I remember, I remember it all—the faces of the women working by my side, nightly scanning our badges at the elevator, doors swinging wide and welcoming us in. We pull sheets off beds, gather towels and washcloths stained and soiled. We pop pills from packages—clonazepam, gabapentin, oxycodone—and when we pass them out it feels like a kind of communion, as if we say *Take, eat.* We walk along the hallway, passing residents' doorways, sometimes knocking, sometimes seeing them and smiling as we go by, sometimes gently waking them from naps and letting them know dinner is ready.

There is a woman whose face and name stay with me—Theresa. One night, while washing Theresa up for bed, I take her stockings off, one by one. I remove her underwear and replace it with a new pair. Then I help her into a nightgown, contorting myself into all kinds of positions to accommodate her.

What happens next, I'll never forget. Theresa grabs my arms, her head nodding involuntarily. "Your little dark arm," she says, patting my skin and smiling. I smile too, searing her face into my memory.

At this point in time, my job becomes a dream. I fall in love with my residents. I sing with them, play bingo with them. I feed them, clean up after them, hold hands with them. I bathe them and I toilet them. And their faces, along with their names, I carry with me. The sweetness of their stories, always with me.

Still, there is one whose memory comes like a haunting.

A Chinese woman, the one who walks with a limp. She stays awake at night—always walking the halls in her nightgown, sitting intrusively close. The women I work with want to watch their late-night TV shows, and here she comes down the hall, limping always, hand pressed on her belly, mumbling "Baby, baby" under her breath.

"Here she comes," they say. "She's crazy, that one. She doesn't know what she's talking about." Every time, I guide her gently back to her room, sparse of any personal items save but one stuffed animal and a brush, I think. I take her back and tuck her in, and I wonder where her family is and why I never see them visit. I wonder where she is from, really from, and when she got here and how.

And I wonder, from the way she walks, if she's ever lost a child. I wonder . . . from the way she holds her belly and mumbles *baby, baby.*

How would you approach this story about the Chinese woman in the nursing home? What would you say to this woman? How would you treat her?

I have not lost a child.* I cannot even type those words without feeling a kind of sorrow fall over me, a sickness filling me up. I am afraid to even write them because seeing them feels too real, too imminent, not at all imaginary. And so I do not know how I will take my mind there, how I will make my way down this deep, dark path to name the nuances, unknown to me, that come with this often dismissed and therefore disenfranchised grief.[2]

I do not know how I will carve out space for the precious babies that never come to full term, or the ones lost to leukemia, or estrangement, or car crashes, or suffocation, or waters too high to rise above. *Yes,* I fear I will fail and fall short in trying to talk about this shared grief and the one thousand ways in which the heart of a parent can be cut open with grief and guilt.

But there is no right way to write about the pain a parent feels when they lose their own child—some to death, some to decisions, some to drugs, some to devastation. I tremble, standing in the chasm of tension that this topic presents. How do you gauge grief, how do you quantify or justify the intensity and validity of what parents feel when they lose children in any way: miscarriage, stillbirth, SIDS, sickness, adoption, abortion, disability, overdose, suicide, kidnapping, death . . . and every other heartbreaking way.

You don't.

You can't.

For, what this book is not, and what I could never do.

Grief cannot be quantified.

There is no scale for sorrows, no way of placing them in order from greatest to least. Every loss is legitimate.

---

* Losing a child is not something I've personally experienced, but it is my biggest fear in life. Which is what led me to write about this topic.

Birth parents experience loss when a child is removed from their home.[3]

There is a sense of disenfranchised grieving for parents whose children died by suicide.[4]

All too often a SIDS death is not socially supported in the way other child deaths are.[5]

The grief of a miscarriage is often forgotten or ignored by others.[6]

Parents of children with special needs experience a unique and more prolonged form of grief.[7]

Our minds cannot grapple with such loss nor handle the shock of it. It is something that should not be, something that goes against what we know to be true, the cycle we see in the natural world. There is birth, *then* there is death. Two separate processes divided by both *chronos* and *kairos* time. Speaking of time: **there is no loss less significant than another**. The one who lost her baby at seven weeks can cry just as real and hard as the one who lost her child at twenty-two years old. There is grace for every parent, including those who've tried but have yet to become parents.

In her article "A Name for a Parent Whose Child Has Died," professor Karla Holloway, author of *Passed On: African American Mourning Stories*, tells the story of the death of her son, along with a critique on culture and our "lack of a word for parents whose child had died."[8] She proposes we find a word for such parents—one that "must be a quiet word, like our grief, but clear in its claim." She begins her search for such a word, and writes that it was "the disorder of a child's death" that led her to lean into the Sanskrit origins of the word *widow*, widely attributed to the specific pain and grief of losing one's husband.

Orphan, too, is a word that gives name to a specific loss, that of parents. Yet it not only defines the primary loss—the death itself—but, because of the cultural awareness brought by the precise definition and therefore meaning of the word, also defines inherent secondary losses: family, home, lifestyle, school, friends, identity . . . the list goes on.

Vilomah, Holloway proposes. Not the "bereaved," not the "grieving parent," but *vilomah*, which means "against a natural order."

"The difference between today's grief and tomorrow's," says Holloway, "is that now there is a name. Vilomah. A parent whose child has died."[9]

What do you think of the significance of giving a loss, such as the loss of a child, a specific name?

The woman on the movie screen groans, that guttural groan that comes before the blood, before the baby. She pushes, harrowing low hums that sigh deep with hurt and hope. She heaves, a syncopated breath. A baby is coming, untangling from the safety of her womb into the big, bright world. One final push, and then she sighs relief. Her baby is born.

She holds the baby. Cradles the baby. Kisses the baby, welcoming this dream on her chest, breathing—and, yet, turning blue. "Give me the baby," says the midwife, insisting an ambulance be called. The baby was fine but now her vitals are falling and she is losing life, slowly, her one, brief breath evanescing.

The baby is born but soon the baby dies—eternally thrusting wife Martha and husband Sean into a spiral of sorrow, all of their losses stacking on the dream of this one. Their future fractures, as does eventually their relationship, as they find themselves falling out of togetherness and into trauma's trajectory. Moreover, as the movie continues the couple find themselves in a legal battle against their midwife, attempting to understand how and why they lost their baby and who was at fault.

There are mixed reviews about this movie, *Pieces of a Woman*, directed by Kornél Mundruczó and written by Kata Wéber, a real-life couple who lost a child themselves. Some say the film is electrifying, some say brutally honest. One movie reviewer writes, "Its effortful grandiosity transforms it into something hollow and even, at times, risible."[10]

In all that is said and thought about this movie, at its intricate core it remains a story of a man and woman who lose a child. Their first child, their only child. Emotions untangle, and a narrative is built around the distinct shattering of two individual lives—the effectual loss of their child.

Before everything crumbles, Sean and Martha pick up a minivan purchased for them by Martha's mother. Though it isn't exactly what they want—for other reasons explored in the movie—they take the vehicle. And of it, Sean ultimately says:

> That's what matters right there. Cloth seats matter. Seat heaters matter. Airbags matter. The three of us matter. It's the tribe that matters. Who cares what she thinks? You know what matters. This is what matters here.[11]

It is not the most profound line in the entire movie. It is, however, precisely prophetic of the unique grief of parents walking through the death of a child. It encapsulates the gravity held by the belief that **every little thing matters**. The dreams matter, the painted nursery matters, the baby showers matter, the ultrasonic images matter, cloth seats matter, airbags in a car matter—Sean and Martha's new van that is big enough for a soon-to-become family of three . . . that matters too. Everything matters, even and especially those things that stretch beyond the baby's birth. Years down the road, dreams of college degrees and graduations, marriages and grandchildren—all of that seems to die when the child dies.

Take a moment to exhale. Then, ponder: What dreams died at the loss of your little loved one(s)?

Pain is in the passing, a grief that comes because they are gone. Pain is in the truth that haunts us: *We couldn't prevent this.* Parental grief groans powerless. And also there is pain in the one million paradoxes, the unassuming, seemingly nonsensical circumstances that surround our losses. Those things in our world that exist together in tension:

Infant and *mortality,* two words that should never go together.[12]
Post-abortion grief of women . . . and men.[13]
Birth parents who grieve placing their children for adoption.[14]
Ambiguous estrangement of a child who lives but relationship is lost.[15]

> The pain isn't just
> in the passing.
>
> The pain is in
> the paradox.

There is pain in not being able to prevent the loss. Parents lament, *If only I'd tried harder, better.* We ache, not only when someone hurts or dies but when pain exists in the midst of possibility. It's almost primitive, like something in us, even if only deep down, knows that this isn't the way things should be.

And for those who feel this, there will always be this gaping hole of guilt and grief, this pang that prompts pondering, places our finger on that one incurable wound.

There is pain in not being able to prevent the loss.

The reminders will be everywhere—in the room, pictures on phones, dates on the calendar. Sometimes the body even remembers before we do.

It is like Taylor Swift's song "Bigger than the Whole Sky," which swept a storm of mothers off their feet when her tenth studio album, *Midnights,* released. In her article "People Who Have Had a Miscarriage Say One Taylor Swift Song Has a Powerful Meaning for Them," Danielle Campoamor writes how the song resonates with those who know of losing their unborn babies. "You were more than just a short time," Taylor sings, her voice airy against synth pads.[16]

These words describe the pain that comes from this one love, this one dream that meant so much but lasted for such a short time. This little life mattered so, especially in the grand scale of how it could and should have been.

It hurts because just as the child becomes—as bones begin and as limbs lengthen—so does the dream. The dream comes as a vision, a hope for who and how this child might become. To lose a child is to lose this too. It is a string of lonely, unseen, ambiguous losses.

What songs help you grieve through loss?

There is no cure for the grief here on earth, no wiping it off, no wishing or willing it away. There is no making small talk of small memories. They will always remain, always reside within. There is no cure—but there is community. There is making space without stigma, joining another's journey without judgment.

> Why does stigma
> still surround
> when stories
> abound?

There is walking with women after abortion. There is hearing the hurting heart of a mom who gave her child away. There is making space for a father's story when he loses his children in a custody battle. There is hearing and honoring the one whose child lives but knows loss due to their diagnosis and disability.

There is admitting to bias and preconceived notions. There is honoring memories and giving language to loss. There is reading and researching, becoming a student of stories. There is making space for the stories we cannot judge because we do not know and therefore cannot hold. There is reframing the questions we ask and making peace with answers we don't want to admit exist.

There is no cure—but there is community.

There is naming the nuance, every layer of grief and guilt stitched. **Say their names**, dare to whisper prayers and confessions for the dream that was. As the syllables leave your lips like prayers lifting high, may you come to believe you are held in this hurt too.

> Liquid leaks,
> watering the ground,
> tears tearing through
> layers of broken earth
> to make a garden grow
> carnations, kissing
> the heart of Mary;
> sorrow of her
> suffering
> Son.

> ———

> The loss isn't little,
> that life no bigger than
> the length of a lemon
> was still a life.
> The dream cradled
> before the diagnosis
> was still a dream.
> The love burning for
> the child before loss
> is still love.

The world will find one thousand ways to crucify you, tell you your mystified grief isn't justified—will have you carry your loss like a secret you should never tell, keep from you the right to claim it broke your heart into a million whispering pieces that echo: *tell it anyway.*

Remember

- Grief cannot be quantified.
- There is no loss less significant than another.
- Every little thing matters.
- Say their names.

Reflect

- How would you approach this story about the Chinese woman in the nursing home? What would you say to this woman? How would you treat her?
- What do you think of the significance of giving a loss, such as the loss of a child, a specific name?
- Take a moment to exhale. Then ponder: What dreams died at the loss of your little loved one(s)?
- What songs help you grieve through loss?

Respire

- Inhale: You've always mattered.
- Exhale: You'll always matter.

Baby's Breath, *Gypsophila*
Meaning: Purity

BABY'S BREATH

for Matrescence

> But what had I gained. . . . A doubtful future, containing only one certainty: that I would become a mother, a role for which I had no earthly preparation. What would become of us—my little girl or boy and its ignorant mother?
>
> Ophelia (Lisa Klein, *Ophelia*)[1]

I wake at 2:30 in the morning with a tightening, the contractions coming in waves—first eight minutes apart, then five, then three. Within two hours I am breathing through a rippling pain that surges through me, nonstop, every two to three minutes for the next thirty hours.

I welcome morphine through an IV drip, feel the cool liquid flush wild into my veins. There is the hand of a nurse on my forehead, the sound of my husband's voice, and my eyes blinking wide, then waiting, then closing shut. When I wake, hours later, I am tired and in a daze, burning with a fever that makes my body a whirlwind of weakness.

I see the faces of strangers, women I do not know but have no choice but to welcome in. I let them be and sit and stand and watch in the presence of my bare and naked body. I hear voices spurring me on as I push. *They don't even know me* and yet they scream for my success, they yell, they cheer, they push me to push this baby who doesn't want to leave my body, who wants to stay right there hugged within me.

I want to remember this feeling, I think. This championing that beckons me to trust. I want to remember this—not the pain or the fear or the needles or my body laid bare for all to see. But the trust. I want to remember sitting on a bed and trusting the one examining my most intimate insides. I want to remember laying out my arm for the needle and trusting that they'd get it right, even if they had to take it out and do it all over again.

I want to remember the person putting medicine in my body, the person injecting the needle near my spine, trusting my husband's whispers beside the bed, trusting the person delivering my baby to safely and sacredly deliver the body that had been created and formed within my own.

It is a whole thirty hours of recklessly letting go of every last bit of control and self-sufficiency I have. No time for fear, no time for backing out. There is only pushing until a life is born and that hollering baby cry is heard, until he is in my arms, until we meet. Until he leaves the safety of my womb for the scary world.

There is a lot of preparation and pushing that need to happen in order to bring life into the home. What have your "preparation" and "pushing" looked like?

Here's a fascinating fact: some mammals can pause their pregnancies, can really postpone the process of fertilized eggs—essentially embryos—developing. I first heard it on *Growing Up Animal*, a documentary series that explores the wonderful, "magical story of a mother's instinct to nurture and her infant's drive to survive."[2]

The number is something like 130 mammal species—including bears, seals, sea lions, and different marsupials—that can, through a process called delayed implantation, prevent a pregnancy from taking place until conditions are just right. This delayed implantation allows a mother's body to delay the development, and therefore birth, of their offspring until they have enough food to sustain them and are in a season with favorable weather and survival conditions.[3]

The series opens by panning through aerials of twenty-five thousand square miles of Canada's Great Bear Rainforest, a pure wilderness home to grizzly bears. Narrator Tracee Ellis Ross opens with a story about Fern, a five-year-old grizzly bear and first-time mom. Fern is a fully grown grizzly but still young in experience, having left her mother only two summers ago.

Facing a fast-approaching winter, she hunts for salmon, finding food not merely to satisfy her hunger but to supplement her changing body. "It's not just her survival at stake, but the promise of new life."[4] The series goes on to document Fern's story as she carries the beginnings of two baby bears. Her body puts off their development and delays their birth. Bypassing winter's cold gives both Fern and her babies a greater chance of survival.

It's a mesmerizing mystery, that **nature knows the nuance of need**. That a bear's body knows what's best, how it can pause a process for the sake of protection, giving time and space for a mama bear to do and be all that she needs. And what of the human body and human babies, and the nuances of our needs? We conceive, cells dancing without delay, giving a mother nine months (at most) when really it seems we could use more sometimes.

It's a sharp transition, going from caring only for yourself to caring for another. Just like Fern, only five years old and yet thrust into motherhood by nature, we too go from being cared for to carrying the weight of another, sustaining them in our bodies—making space for them in our homes—and caring so much about their survival. Our bodies change, cells collecting, hormones raging, skin stretching. Our lives and schedules change. Our homes change. Our relationships change. Our emotions change. The world is not the same; it is altogether new, a novel and captivating force.

When a baby is born, or when we foster or adopt a child into our heart and home, not only is there new life but also there is new loss. The word *matrescence* gives name to this nuance, defining this ambiguous crossover from womanhood into motherhood. When a woman brings a baby into her world, every conversation centers on that baby, that child. We celebrate because a baby is born, has come home, *yes*.

But so, too, is a mother born.[5]

> *We go from being cared for to caring for others. What comes to mind when you think of this transition?*

One of my favorite stories that involves matrescence is that of a motherless girl who falls in love with a prince. The prince and the girl find themselves in a forbidden love, which only further complicates as a cascade of deceit and betrayal enter their beloved kingdom. With poignant reimagining and retelling, author Lisa Klein takes an infamous tragedy that ends in a royal bloodbath and reimagines its ending, recasting the role of this female character through an alternate conclusion focused on redemption rather than revenge.

Through this retelling, this female character, historically criticized for her unfortunate fate—doomed by drowning—is revived, even redeemed. Murder gives way to madness in every rendition of Shakespeare's *Hamlet*, from the original play, written at the turn of the seventeenth century, to the 1990 movie with director Mel Gibson in the title role, along with Glenn Close as Queen Gertrude and Helena Bonham Carter as Ophelia, to the 1996 film starring Kenneth Branagh (also the film's director) as Hamlet and Kate Winslet as Ophelia. In all of these versions, madness is the makeup of these characters in combustion. And it is their unfortunate, inevitable downfall to death.

Lisa Klein's young adult book, *Ophelia*, isn't just some flimsy, flippant attempt at fiction. Through the literal revival of Ophelia (in

Klein's retelling, Ophelia doesn't die but merely feigns her death), Klein also gives voice to a critical, cultural revival of Ophelia as a symbolic literary character, mainly in regard to a woman's position, power, and agency. Klein unearths reimagined interior motives for Ophelia by raising the stakes of survival. She officially seals the love between Ophelia and Hamlet with "the deed of love itself" and a secret ceremony to exchange vows.[6] Soon after, Ophelia discovers she is pregnant with Hamlet's heir.

In *Ophelia*, instead of taking her life, Ophelia saves it, feigning her suicide by using her knowledge of herbs and flowers. Her story continues and Ophelia, narrating the story herself, sets out to "dispel the darkness about me and cast a light upon the truth"[7] of the sacrifices she makes to sustain the life of her baby as well as her own.

In all of this, we see an orphaned young woman who loses love, falls in love, loses love again, and gives birth to love—all in the tender years of her becoming in body and psyche. She is on a tightrope taut with tension as she transitions into motherhood. In more ways than one, she must and will change. Klein does this by rewriting Ophelia's madness as a meticulous, motherly strategy. Instead of a bloody ending filled with death, she brings a bloody ending brought forth by birth. Ophelia gives birth to a boy, and a new layer of maturity is unearthed within her. She comes of age and all at once reckons with the loss laced in her life. "This, then, is the fruit of it all," she says to herself. "Not the punishment of death, but the gift of life."[8]

Ophelia has given birth to a beautiful boy but also succumbs to her own birth as a new layer of maturity and motherliness develops and is unearthed within her.

> There is beauty in this birth too.
> Not all breaking. Not all broken tears.

For the millions of births that take place each year in the United States alone, there still isn't much conversation on the change that comes with matrescence. Erin Zimmerman writes, in her article

"The Identity Transformation of Becoming a Mom," of her own journey through matrescence:

> Without the vocabulary to describe what I was experiencing, I was left feeling like a stranger in my own body, both literally and metaphorically; my body had changed, but I didn't really know my life anymore, either. I loved my daughter—so much it scared me—but chafed at the loss of so many freedoms.[9]

And she is not the only one. Despite the mere ninety thousand posts on Instagram tagged with #matrescence, the conversation on this topic still skims the surface. Matrescence is only just becoming a word in the mouths of women and mothers everywhere. Of motherhood, and the changes it brings, it's more common to speak of expanding waistlines rather than other lines—the boundaries of our souls that, if we're honest, seem to shrink and swell to shapes and sizes different from when we first began. It's another disenfranchised grief, really, so easily eclipsed by the grand entrance of a new child.

This transition to motherhood is a tug and a pull that surges, bringing change and influx not merely to a woman's waist and weight but her whole self—emotionally, mentally, physically, spiritually, and socially. And like adolescence, matrescence is an ongoing process that comes in layers and lasts for years. It is sustained, stretching into the mothering of "young children or adolescents, and then also emerging adults, and then the empty-nest experience."[10]

This transition to motherhood is a tug and a pull that surges.

I can't help but think about that first day I left the hospital with my newborn in my arms. I took the elevator down one hundred floors and walked the halls of one thousand doors, and slipped into my car and just took off with this new baby. I felt like I was committing some heist, like I was taking something I had no business taking. Though I gained something that day, my hands filled to the brim with life overflowing, I swear I lost something that day too. Something fell off me in that hospital bed, those white sheets soaked with my blood and sweat, sheets that cradled me in my becoming, washed one thousand times over for the next woman and the next one.

> We heave,
> then leave
> with more
> than when
> we first
> began.

A woman emerges from the womb herself, thrust new and afraid into the world of motherhood. Adoptive and foster moms especially know this, as they are thrust into motherhood in a matter of days or hours. We are not spared from the blow of it, the blunt fall from a small and safe world into all that looms large. Suddenly another life, for which we give thanks, breathes at the expense of our own, and the demand is costly. Perhaps that is what psychiatrist Daniel Stern means when he says that "giving birth to a new identity can be as demanding as giving birth to a baby."[11] There is loss, indeed, and consequently grief, because what is familiar falls away and fades into something foreign.

There is the weight of worry, knowing life—this new life in the way of the world, the way of love.

> We swell,
> all size and
> soul and
> strain.

> All messy
> all worn
> all stretched
> all caving in.

We carry
all, even as
we cradle
one.

There is a tug-of-war, and we are held at the center of two opposing paths—who we were and who we are becoming. There isn't enough time or space to process it all, to realize that this, too, is a loss worth grieving, a giving of what was for what is and is to become. Our hips have widened, our pelvic bones have shifted, our homes have shifted, and our hearts have swelled. And they occupy our thoughts—that space once reserved for dreams and hopes and things. What is left of us is our will—the want and need to make sense of it all, to make meaning of it.

In what ways do you feel different from your younger self? In what ways do you feel the same?

About two years after I had my first son, I found myself thinking about these exact things. On May 19, 2019, I wrote on Instagram:

It occurred to me late last evening, as the Carolina sun slipped into hiding and while I swept leaves off the front patio and misted the white mandevilla vine that creeps tall along the trellis, that this is fun for me. Toil—unobligated, unnecessary toil—is fun for me. Somewhere in between the elongation of my body and the widening of my hips, I became something other than what was when I first began. I am no longer a young girl with lanky, long legs, brushing back unruly hair on toy dolls, talking myself through dressing Barbie to look breathtaking and beautiful for her imaginary dream date. The heart of this she-child still resides within me, just under the surface, whereas the glimmer of dreams as possible, tangible, able realities still seduces my woolgathering mind, my hopeful soul. But this is also true: I am a woman—in physical frame, and psychologically fierce in passion and desire and want and need and delighted pleasure. And it just fascinates me that what captures my heart these days is a different kind of indulgence—the way a vine blossoms, or a patterned rug, or a working vacuum, or a sliver of chocolate pressed against the inside of my cheek and melting, under the weight of a speechless tongue.[12]

It is just as L'Engle writes: "I am every other age I have been."[13] Though much is lost, much remains. Though much changes, much sustains. Though much is hidden, much is unearthed. Though much remains unfinished, much is developed.

Motherhood makes a muddied mess of you, untidies all the perfectly placed pieces that once held together your life from the center. This mess of life is the masterpiece of love. Maybe it isn't so much a falling apart as it is a falling away of the things that once concerned you. It's a delicate balance—holding their world as you hold your own. Spinning your world as you spin theirs too.

> Dainty dream of
> baby's breath
> changed the body
> she had left,
> stretched the
> home that
> fit so well,
> grew the heart
> to surge and
> *swell.*

———

> I wear stains more than I wear smiles.
> Like a smock that mocks,
> motherhood makes a mess of me.
> I wake, I stretch long limbs,

I hurl hurry into the humble faces before me, and
I dress in all my discontent:
I slip on socks of sorrow,
put on pants with pockets
big and wide and deep enough
to hold all of my disappointments.
I pull a sweater, two sizes too big,
over my head and it swallows me whole,
my whole fragile frame
made weak by the mundane.
Steady hands reach to enfold—
a cup—a kind calm to coat my throat for every
loud and rageful sound that lingers, like
intolerance on the tongue, and all the tired,
and tears, too, that fell, finding
familiar grooves and tracing my
silhouette, the still-soaked curve
that carries all my complaint,
all my lament, all my losses—
named and numbered, one by one by one.
And it is only dawn, the day still yawning,
and yet I am grasping for a thread of truth
in all these lengths and layers,
this remnant of reminders, telling me
my rags are worth more
than all the world's riches,
worth more than all the silk gowns
and diamond-stitched crowns.
Worth it for every smile stretched
ear to ear to ear—
yes, even mine—
though I wear stains more than smiles.
My smock that mocks,
motherhood made a new dress for me.[14]

———

**You will not
bounce back.**
You will
fall forward,
loving through
your loss. Yes,
even this one.

Remember

- Nature knows the nuance of need.
- A woman emerges from the womb herself, thrust new and afraid into the world of motherhood.
- Motherhood makes a muddied mess of you.
- You will not bounce back.

Reflect

- There is a lot of preparation and pushing that need to happen in order to bring life into the home. What have your "preparation" and "pushing" looked like?
- We go from being cared for to caring for others. What comes to mind when you think of this transition?
- In what ways do you feel different from your younger self? In what ways do you feel the same?

Respire

- Inhale: I make space for new life.
- Exhale: I make space for me.

Azalea, *Rhododendron*
Meaning: Fragility

AZALEA

for Suicide

In seven days, God created the world. And in seven seconds,
I shattered mine.

Ben Thomas (*Seven Pounds*)[1]

The call comes, a ringing to jolt me out of the bliss of the day's
bright pouring through sheer-framed windows. There he
is, our son, cradled in layers of baby-soft blankets, smiling and, when not smiling, yawning. And when he is not smiling or
yawning, he is just breathing, just being. He is all but seven days old,
and we are head over heels, altogether in over our heads, and in love.

My husband holds a Canon 40D, adjusts the lens to focus on our
son's nose and newborn feet, his hair, and his hands so perfectly
clasped. He is a tender thing, and we want to capture this on camera.
The essence of his sweetness, the sweetness of his life.

My phone rings, and I answer only to hear my mother breaking
down on the other end. She rambles without making sense in her
tone or her words, something along the lines of *It's really bad* and *He
didn't make it*. Words slip through like sand between fingers. I cannot
catch them all, cannot grasp what she's said. I feel my breath break

like hers, inhaling slow and long and hard and fast, and exhaling all the same. Her fragmented breath tells me what her words cannot, what I don't want to know. Someone is dead. Someone who means a lot to us. Someone we love. *Who is it?* I want to know, want to make sense of what is chaotic and crumbling.

She groans his name, says it was a gun and that he didn't make it. I ask her for more, ask her to tell me the horrible things I do not want to know, all the horrible things I wish were untrue, because how could suicide come by a bullet breaking through body and brain when there is a newborn baby in the room lying blissfully unaware, peacefully asleep in the softest blankets?

I hang up the phone. I do not cry, cannot conjure up a tear, because I am stuck in suspended thought. It is a conglomeration of *why* and *how.* Why this way, why anyway? Hadn't we just seen him months earlier? Smiling, happy, whole, here. *How* haunts the most, though. *How did the bullet hit?* I imagine the bullet breaking through skin, the whole scene playing out in my mind as if I were there or something. I see his side profile, see his tear-soaked cheeks, the doubt of existence spinning a wild storm in the iris of his eye. I hear the gunshot, feel it pierce like fire passing through the path of my heart, and see this replay over and over, that bullet splintered into a million masses, just like my heart at the hearing of this.

Has suicide ever touched your life in any way? Name your nuance—there is space for your story.

The Suicide Prevention Resource Center reports that 53 percent of all suicides happen by way of firearms.[2] Rutgers University reports that approximately 90 percent of suicide attempts involving a firearm result in death, compared to less than 5 percent of attempts by all other methods combined.[3] Rutgers also adds that those who die by suicide by means of firearms are more likely to talk about suicide in the month before ending their lives.[4]

How can this be, though, since my memory takes me to a baby shower, right there in Paramus, New Jersey? It is my baby shower, and I am surrounded by family and friends, all the faces I find love and comfort in. And there he is, the one we lost too soon, just like everyone else—smiling and hugging and laughing and loving.

The memory paints the picture that he is fine, more than fine. There we were, just two months before I gave birth, two months and seven days before he lost his life to suicide. Should I have known, then, to ask him how he was doing, *really doing*? Should I have known to tell him he could call if anything came up, *anything at all*? How could I have known, when there was no talk of guns, or bridges, or blades on skin—no talk of suffering and no talk of pain beneath his smile, no signs at all?

Now, years later, I am still suspended, still baffled by the truth that breaks through numbers on graphs and charts.

> Data tells the stories
> we dare not
> discover.
>
> Silent suffering
> summons
> self-infliction, of which
>
> guns grant
> a guarantee
> of g o n e.

The ones with guns really want an end to the suffering, really want the pain to stop. They really want a way out, a way to leave their wounds behind. They want something, anything, to shoot through the sorrow and break through all that feels and is bad. They want to end the pain with no chance of it persisting.

Where is the statistic that tells us how much our words would have mattered, how much we could have changed the trajectory of brass bullets? Where are the numbers to tell us we can save the ones who feel like they want to die? What is the secret to soothing the ones who suffer in silence, surrounded by an invisible fog of gasoline fumes?

Chills cover my body when I think back to the moment my mother called me, and the months that followed. Suicide slipped into our family, seeped in, making a place in our story while I cradled new life in my hands—the relentless cycle, the paradox of pain in paradise.

There is a haunting that hovers when the loss is that of suicide. There is shock and disbelief, there is confusion and clamoring to find the missing pieces of the puzzle, shattered and strewn. There is guilt, all the many memories that play on repeat, taunting you and telling you the one hundred ways you could have seen this coming, as if you could have stopped the bullet, as if you could have stopped the blood from seeping out onto the clean carpet, onto the cold pavement. There is this weight of *what if*, and you never know just how the pain will seep in and out of you until it happens to you. You'll never know the length of your cry or the depth of your denial until you get that call.

What makes suicide difficult to walk through is not only the loss of our loved ones but living through the stereotypes and stigmas that still exist around suicide. There are so many phrases seared into our vocabulary. *Suicide is the ultimate sin*, we hear, echoing always. We look for the sin in the story but hardly ever the suffering beneath the surface.

> Do not belittle
> bodies lost by
> way of bullets,
>
> souls
> suffocated
> by string,
>
> pain pacified
> with piles
> of pills.

Love them
in memory
in mourning
in message.

*What would it look like to create compassionate spaces where
stories of suicide are safe to share?*

The film *Seven Pounds* is filled with plot potholes, some say, and
criticized as being far from acclaimed. But still it is a nuanced narra-
tive that is the stuff of real life. And, at its core, perhaps it resonates
with the same magnitude of the tragedy it intends to mirror. In the
movie, written by Grant Nieporte and directed by Gabriele Muccino,
protagonist Ben Thomas, as played by Will Smith, is a man drown-
ing in guilt and grief. Seven lives are lost at the fault of his own, and
he is forever marred by the memory of their deaths. He commits to
following through with a plan to make retribution for the lives lost,
as well as, perchance, seek some sort of redemption for himself.

He sets out to make sense of these seven deaths by donating his
organs to save the lives of seven strangers, those he deems worthy
of a second chance, the second chance he seemingly won't give him-
self. His act of philanthropy, however, is nothing less than punish-
ment, the only way he sees through his heavy weight of *what ifs*.
Ben Thomas's grief ultimately portrays his deeply embedded morals
and set of beliefs—that he is irredeemable and that what he did is
unforgivable and ultimately unbearable. He'll give seven "pounds"
of himself to pay the debt of seven deaths.

The film opens with Ben Thomas on a call with a 911 dispatcher.
He is weak and speaks with strain and through obvious pain. He's
calling in his own suicide. The scene is a prolepsis, a flash forward
of which the rest of the movie will unravel its meaning. The line
immediately following this moment is of some reflective, dreamlike
scene in which a voice-over from Ben plays. He is swimming, and

in a voice-over he says: "In seven days, God created the world. And in seven seconds, I shattered mine."[5]

Already, just one minute into the movie, a jarring conflict drenched with dissonance is established and is sustained throughout, right down to the movie's soundtrack, which features the song "The Crisis" composed by Ennio Mariconne. During a love scene, "The Crisis" comes to a crescendo and vamps throughout with a sustained sound that intrusively interrupts its own melody as well as the movie scene. Of this song, a reviewer wrote:

> A simple, dogmatic loop of an arpeggiated D major add 9 chord which strikes both the minor and major 3rd to create a poignant sound that disturbs an otherwise peaceful and beautiful melody . . . this inclusion of both the minor and major 3rd is a profound representation of both the beauty and tragedy's (sic) that exists in each person's life.[6]

This song musically embodies paradox and dissonance, a tapestry of beauty and tragedy that is not only Ben's life but life itself. It strikes the chord that loss is inevitable. Loss can occur at any moment, even amid what is loved and lovely. Loss lingers, though we want and will to forget it, leave it behind. In seven seconds, one accident rips through all Ben ever loved. For Ben, then, the only way forward is what comes next.

In seven seconds, he'll end his life to end his loss.

If you had seven seconds to tell someone how much their life mattered, who would you tell and what would you tell them?

Grief undulates. It is evasive and invisible. Unnamable and untamable.

I cannot find enough words to string together sentences spun with all the guttural intention in the world to capture all there is to it. Cannot tell you why the one you loved suffered in this way, or

146

what statistic they fit into or when or how it might have happened. There is no one, real way to define death by suicide. Stories will always slip between the cracks of statistics.

Was it guilt or was it grief?

Was it trauma or was it fear?

Was it a mistake or was it intentional?

Was it pain or was it debt?

Was it rage or was it sorrow?

I am still reeling in the questions of my own story, of which I will never know the answer, see the full picture, or have clarity or closure. What is for certain, though, is that loss by way of suicide leaves the living with more losses. Yes, **loss lingers in the wake of life left too soon**. We inherit the guilt and grief they leave behind, it seems. We continue on, carrying *the crisis*, the dissonance that comes with their death etched into our days. We hold the questions and we hold the complexity, just like I did on March 8, 2019, when I wrote the following:

> They say all wounds heal in time, and that the sting of death fades in its passing. They lied. Because the wound your death has left will always seep with fresh, red blood. It hurts, every time. And the complexity of your leaving us will never hold a thread thick enough to close the gap that cut through our hearts the day we heard you passed. I remember you, in moments when the silence hits hard in my soul. . . . I miss you—and if I could have had just one more day with you that's what I would tell you. That I didn't realize you could miss a person more than you thought you loved them.[7]

The little loss is in the complexity of their leaving, all the birthdays for which they'll never again blow out candles. The little loss is in the small reminders that pass. It's in all the ways their death is diminished by a society that still, after all these years, holds a stigma that stains the story, steals the rightful sorrow of those who mourn. The little loss is in the one thousand ways culture cuts, blithely boasting that a theology of salvation matters more than a theology of suffering.

I want to tell you what you might already know, what I have found to be true as I've lived through the loss of a loved one to suicide. The sheer shock you feel comes as it should, because this death was unnatural, untimely, and cannot be undone. You will feel, if you do not already, a violation of your privacy while police investigate and friends interrogate. And you will lose the security, the sense of sanctuary, you once knew. You won't know what to say, how to tell the story, how to make sense of it to strangers sending sympathetic messages across social platforms. You don't have to, by the way. Don't have to make it make sense. You will struggle to know what to do with the items they've left behind, how to tell the kids and cousins. You will want to protect their reputation, want to guard against ripples of rumors, all cuts and stings that add to the loss.

You will seek out space to sit and gather your grief, searching for circles, searching for churches, searching for classroom doors cracked open after school hours, and I hope these places and spaces do help you gauge your grief, both the weight of it and all the ways it matters.

> Azalea, the fragility of flowers,
> is bright and bold with color,
> will turn your head, enchant
> you to see beauty instead of
> what's beneath the surface, still,
> we see your shallow roots,
> needy and temperamental,
> prone to overwatering,
> drowning. It's what you
> do, not who you are,
> never mind the poison
> in your petals.
> Don't you know?

Your soul is
evergreen.
And we
love
you
as
you
are.

———

If I had known that you felt this numb, your mind
slipping manic, moments unmirrored in the façade
forced through your many faces. I might have looked
you in the eye, held you pinned down under the weight
of some unconjurable strength. Screamed sonnets at the
fated stars, drank the cup with you. Anything, to make
you feel just a fraction of the good in all the guise of grief,
make you taste on your tongue a flicker of light in all the
damned darkness. Maybe you could have burned the
world down, built it anew, just the way you wanted. If I
had known you felt this numb, I might have looked you
in the eye, made you feel just a fraction of the good in all
the guise of grief.

———

The world loves you,
and the world loses
if it loses you.

———

We want to know
of your pain
and of your plans
to end it.

We want to hear
the horrors you have seen,
hold you as you heave
confessions of the horrible
things you know.

Tell us of the graves
you fantasize about
giving yourself over to,
of your grief buried
in the ground.

Heave every heavy thing
here on this hanging earth,
suspended in the space
between heaven and hell
where we are ever with you.

Remember

- Grief undulates.
- Loss lingers in the wake of life left too soon.
- The world loves you.

Reflect

- Has suicide ever touched your life in any way? Name your nuance—there is space for your story.
- What would it look like to create compassionate spaces where stories of suicide are safe to share?
- If you had seven seconds to tell someone how much their life mattered, who would you tell and what would you tell them?

Respire

- Inhale: You are remembered.
- Exhale: You are missed.

Hyssop, *Hyssopus*
Meaning: Cleanliness

HYSSOP
for Plagues

All things to end are made,
The plague full swift goes by;
I am sick, I must die.
Lord, have mercy on us!

Thomas Nashe, "A Litany
in Time of Plague"[1]

I'd tell you how it happened, how the world came burning down, but you already know. You were there too. You have your own story, your own glittering version of what happened. For as long as we live, the memories will never leave us.

I remember when I first heard of a contagion causing quarantine cases in Seattle, Washington. On I-485, I was making my way home on the loop from East Charlotte to I-77 North, listening to Charlotte's NPR news station. The woman on the radio spoke of people in Seattle with symptoms and in self-isolation, and of neighbors delivering dinner, but nothing of pandemics, nothing the public need yet panic.

I remember feeling a fleeting sense of ease entangled with empathy. A sense of compassion for Seattle devoid of any concern, even the slightest bit, for the future, or that this contagion, this corona-virus, could spread itself far and wide like a wildfire, from Wuhan to Washington and all over the world.

But life changes in the instant. *The ordinary instant.*[2] In any instant, the world we know can shatter. Not the world from history textbooks slipped thick between our hands, but our right-now, twenty-first-century world. Quickly, collectively, COVID-19 splintered the world, taking with it every preconceived sense of safety. We've lost lives left and right, caught under the cut and sting of a global shard driving in deep until it's felt by the whole body, not one place immune.

We weep
Together

We're weak
Together

It takes weeks of weeping while slicing sausage and crying into the cowlick of my son's curly hair and staring up at the stillness of an insentient ceiling—past twelve, past one, past two o'clock in the morning—for me to make sense of the arithmetic, the insurmountable equations erupting from this pandemic.

The subtraction of it all, the lives lost from lungs failing to the faint push of breath and air. That one, precious life, George Floyd, lost from breath bound beneath the brutality of an unapologetic, bent knee—a death so representative of generations of Black bodies held in restraint under the same kind of repressive knee. Then there's the loss of tens of millions of careers that crumbled while the market caved in.

The division of it all, division of us as we typed and "liked" our way through life on touch screens, reducing ourselves to the lowest, most common denominators, doing long division in long distance with figures and factors like indifference, indignation, and fear. This disease did more than take life. It shed light on the divides and disparities that plague our people.

The multiplication of it all—the protests, the police brutality, the politics, and the pandemic are only proof of our propensity to perpetually pin ourselves one against another.

The addition of it all—what does all of this mean for the grand sum of our lives? Despite seeing the wreckage of a violent virus, still the most active and aggressive agent to replicate and reproduce within us is not COVID-19 but the apathy and abhorrence in our beating hearts, our breath. The maskless words we type and think bring decline and death in uncompassionate measure. Our world spins dizzy on its divided axis while hashtags pile up and headlines read like canons of eulogies.

Yes, it takes weeks of weeping for me to realize the impact of it all, the numbers creeping high as the names on our newsfeeds scroll like etchings on tombs of stone, like front-page stories fresh in New York newsstands. Too soon forgotten.

Too soon to be forsaken.

> *What are the hard memories you cradle from any instance of global tension or collective suffering?*

Collective grief is the name for this—for the way we react to any weight that wrecks more worlds than one.[3] This is the name for the pain held in the chest when lives are lost by the hundreds of thousands. When bombs fall from the void of dark skies, prompting prayers of terror on the trembling lips of all people.

> Grief is a thread
> in the tapestry
> of man,
>
> keeping us
> tethered,
> tight knit,
> together.

Grief is both personal and universal. It is as wide as it is deep. It expands from country to country, right into the animal kingdom. Animals know this kind of gathered grief too. Wild African elephants return to the remains of their dead.[4] Giraffes show signs of distress when they stand over and near their dead.[5] Then there are the painted wolves that sing. Nick Lyon, a producer and director of the documentary series *Dynasties*, and his crew came across a pack of painted wolves doing something that had never been recorded before:

> The pack of painted wolves had been left without a leader, which is unusual. Normally, leaders are ousted and replaced by their challenger, but this particular pack's matriarch, Tait, had died unexpectedly. Several months after Tait's death, the wolves started to pair up into male/female couples and howl together in a duet. While not exactly the same noise, it was similar to the cry they use when one of the pack goes missing.[6]

"It was a magical feeling," says Lyon, talking about this moment when he and his crew happened upon this singing pack of painted wolves.[7] More research, I'm sure, will come of this to confirm exactly what prompted this pack to sing. But this is certain: animals sense when something is not right. Animals, too, can sense when their world has been wrecked, turned upside down by disorder and death. It is an echo of the many ways we humans embody grief and how we carry it collectively.

> Grief gathers
> Man *and* Grief
> gathers Animals
> alike.

And like wild African elephants returning to the remains of their dead and touching the bones with their trunks, or painted wolves singing in the witness of other painted wolves, grief begs to be carried collectively. It begs to be touched and shared and heard and held.

I remember the first days of the COVID-19 pandemic, how they stretched into weeks and then months, then disappeared into years. I, like countless others, waited for the world to weep collective tears at the sheer number of lives being lost, as well as other ambiguous losses.

I waited—mask, mandates, and all—to hear more than prayers and platitudes. More than complaints about the small inconveniences such a devastating tragedy had made in our communities. When I look back, I am affirmed that the plea wasn't all in my head. Headlines tell the story that other humans demanded just the same:

"More Than 250,000 Are Dead. Why Is There So Little Collective Grief?"[8]

"Collectively, We're Grieving Far More Than COVID-19 Deaths, Say Experts"[9]

"Coronavirus Today: Where's America's Shared Grief?"[10]

The unique impact of this pandemic was the shutting down and the social distancing—the separation. And while separation was (and for some still is) necessary, it also took away the most powerful tool available to us—community.

Trauma intensified for every one of us because of our loss of togetherness, loss of rituals of grieving. Funerals and vigils altogether died or became so severely reconstructed that they looked and felt unrecognizable to the rituals we knew by heart.

Grief knows no terrain,
grief stretches across
topographic lines
and travels through
timelines.

What does community mean to you? What would happen if you lost that?

I once learned that the use of *adieu* in Shakespeare's plays will sometimes signal a character's final farewell, not only within that particular scene but within the whole script. "Adieu, adieu, adieu, remember me," says the ghost of Hamlet's father after he tells of his tragedy, and then he is no more.[11] "Dry sorrow drinks our blood. Adieu, adieu!" says Romeo, his last time speaking to Juliet while they are both still alive.[12]

Adieu, because it just might be the last time we'll see this character. Not just a goodbye or a see you later. But *adieu* as in the foreshadowing of an unfortunate fate, most often ending in death.

I share this to pave the way for a particular poem's first line. As it goes, "A Litany in Time of Plague" by Shakespearean contemporary Thomas Nashe begins:

> Adieu, farewell, earth's bliss;
> This world uncertain is.[13]

Adieu. This time the word comes not from a fictional ghost or star-crossed lovers but from a man writing from the experience of living out a long and drawn-out collective adieu—a plague. The poem begins with *adieu* because that word would be at the forefront of Elizabethan London's collective mind, would it not? Written for Nashe's play *Summer's Last Will and Testament*, this poem was "performed privately around the summer of 1592 when plague closed London's public theaters."[14]

A poem (within a play) is written about a plague. The play (and therefore poem) are performed privately. The private performances are a result of plague. The plague closed theaters in the summer of 1592.

This all feels very familiar to the pandemic of 2020. People of the twenty-first century are not the only or the first to carry and come through collective grief. The nature of "A Litany in Time of Plague" is grim, as it should be, for it is the outpour of one stricken with sickness:

> The plague full swift goes by;
> I am sick, I must die.

There are other lines that abound with the resonance of suffering. Of inevitable endings, Nashe writes:

> Physic himself must fade.
> All things to end are made.

And of the invincibility of mortality, he writes:

> Brightness falls from the air;
> Queens have died young and fair.

And yet while these sorrow-filled stanzas are widely relatable, both for Elizabethan Londoners and our modern selves, there is another grounding force that exists within this poem—one that satisfies the poem's very title. Six times throughout the poem, the plea appears: "Lord, have mercy on us!"

In his article "Poetry for a Time of Plague," Steve Mentz compares Nashe's depiction of illness to the shared suffering experienced by and through COVID-19. The unifying factor in Nashe's poem is not solely the subject of suffering, the common ground of people bidding adieu to earth and world and life. Rather, it's the litany—all six lines of "Lord, have mercy on us!" It is communal words, not just communal wounds, that stitch souls together in strength. It's communal movement, action, expression, and prayer that bring us together, bond us together.

Our national community, leaderless and frightened, has not yet found a shared song to mourn our building losses. We might do worse than recall the cadences of Nashe's Litany. Lord, have mercy on us![15]

> Litany gives
> language
>
> invokes the
> voice
>
> of many
> made one.

Even when theaters shut down and plagues rage. When churches close and schools stop students at the door. We need songs, like the painted wolves do. We need prayers and poems that prompt an outpouring of all pain and all we profess to be true. We need liturgies and litanies, collective ways to carry our laments, the language of our loss.

Do you have a favorite poem that's carried you through hard times? How has it strengthened you?

Here is what deeply matters about collective grief: mourning can make way for memory making. Grief is not a thing to just get through; it's not a race to heal from history. Rather, the way of grief is to carry the weight of history into the present. **We keep memories like close companions,** our trauma like a teacher, guiding us and leading us forward. We would be machines if we didn't make meaning out of memories. We would be computers, storing information and erasing data, heartless, cold, and calculated.

> We are mortals.
> We hold memory.
> We were made to feel
> not merely made to be fixed.

A common question regarding collective suffering that I heard a lot when growing up, probably because of my proximity to New York City, was the one about why it seems that only "hard times" bring people together. I was attending a middle school just twenty minutes outside of New York City in 2001. How close we were to the planes that hit the towers that day. In my mind, I can still see faces filled with fear. I can feel the confusion and chaos of it, all of us children gathered in the locked cafeteria as the rumors murmured.

But my body and my brain also remember the coming together. I remember, vaguely, hearing stories of kindness and camaraderie. Like the kind you'd find at Christmastime, a spirit that sees and lends and lingers with people just a little bit longer.

It's called *solidarity*—maybe that's what, when named, shared grief can and does give way to. On the webpage for the 9/11 Memorial & Museum, I read, "The urge to mourn alongside others brought people together throughout New York City, across the country, and around the world. . . . Spontaneous memorials appeared in town squares, on roadside billboards, and outside firehouses and police stations."[16]

This is what we lost when COVID-19 came. Like Nashe, we lost the stage. We lost connection with our communities, and connections still remain lost—one of the many ambiguous losses that lingers in ambivalence.

> However hard it
> is to find
> safety in a
> circle—I hope
> you find it.
> Slowly, surely,
> building anew
> *budding* again.

Have you ever experienced a moment or season of solidarity? What was it for and how did it make you feel?

Can you feel what your neighbor feels, without question, without hesitation? Can you feel the weight of their tears, fathom the history of their trauma? Can you imagine the weight carried in their collective bones to the point that you physically make a sound, a movement, reacting in such a way that the burden has to escape from you somehow, someway?

This is the kind of compassion that chips away at what is broken within. Never curing the physical pain completely but curing that plague of apathy that rages within, restoring us to love the ones we share life with.

> I hope you feel
> surrounded as your
> grief is shared.
>
> I hope you find
> space that's safe
> to feel.
>
> I hope you find
> hands to hold
> what hurts.
>
> And I hope you
> give these things, too.

I consider this concept of solidarity universally, but I consider it personally too. This has been true of my life. A little girl growing to see grief through the eyes of her father. I hold the memory of a man I've never met, my father's father, because of compassionate strangers gathering to honor what should have been.

A man, a cop, murdered in the quaintest, quietest town, whose story and sacrifice pulled on the city like a center of gravity.

Every year, in the same place at the same time, they gathered. Collected in grief, memory, sound, speech, and prayer. They told me the stories I needed to know and they wanted to hear again themselves. *He drove his patrol car all around town checking in on the kids. He'd stop in for lunch with friends.* Once, someone held my hand or hugged me, I can't remember who or which, and reminisced that he would sometimes buy presents for the kids in the neighborhood whom he knew might not find any under their Christmas trees.

I've heard rumors he cooked for the guys at the police station, that he was always happy and smiling—always in a "chipper" mood. As a young girl, just tall enough to reach, I'd hold my father's hand and watch as the men in stiff uniforms marched past with scary weapons. I remember the sound of gunshots followed by clouds of smoke and the procession of drums and bagpipes as metal shells hit the ground in solidarity and in honor of him, the grandfather I never met.

> Holding hyssop,
> this we pray
> purge us of this
> pain that plagues,
> the body, mind
> and spirit too.
> Holy herb that
> heals us whole,
> restore these
> broken hearts
> for you.
>
> ———

He is the blood, and you,
you are standing under Israel's door post
protected from the plague, but still
with nightmares of the Nile running rampant
in your reminiscent mind, a royal
bloodbath of the gods at war,
red and thick like the blood
beneath your bones, death swimming
in the current of life
unquenchable.

———

**Collective grief
is the communal cry
that what shattered
mattered.**

Remember

- We weep *together.*
- Grief is both personal and universal.
- We keep memories like close companions.
- Collective grief is the communal cry that what shattered mattered.

Reflect

- What are the hard memories you cradle from any instance of global tension or collective suffering?
- What does community mean to you? What would happen if you lost that?

- Do you have a favorite poem that's carried you through hard times? How has it strengthened you?
- Have you ever experienced a moment or season of solidarity? What was it for and how did it make you feel?

Respire

- Inhale: Lord.
- Exhale: Have mercy on us.

Snowdrop, *Galanthus*
Meaning: Consolation

SNOWDROP

for Death

I never wanted to go away, and the hard part now is the leaving you all. I'm not afraid, but it seems as if I should be homesick for you even in heaven.

Beth March (Louisa May Alcott, *Little Women*)[1]

The world is in the thick of a second wave, numbers swelling again, disease and death leaving bodies in their wake, taking souls by the hundreds of thousands, taking the soul of a man I know and love by name and by heart. I write about it right after it happened:

> This is the part where I rip my heart wide open, invite you deep in the farthest corner, sit you down and tell you about how we lost him to COVID-19, lost him because his body was broken and it was time to let it lay in rest. Lost him because his lungs could no longer pump breath to the blood beneath his beautiful bronze skin. We lost his body but not his burning love, that kind of love that brought him with bags of groceries to the back doors of our homes.[2]

I am eight months pregnant and the world is in the swell of a surge of COVID-19 cases, and I have no choice but to watch the funeral of my grandfather, my mother's father, through the screen on my computer.

> If only screens
> could scream.

It's like I'm nine years old again, in that room with a casket and *one hundred gawking, teary eyes*. It's like I'm looking at my grandfather, or what appears to be him. His face through the screen looks so foreign and yet so familiar. I wait, listening for him to emerge with prayer, erupt with stories to keep us all day and all night. But there is no sound, nothing of the man I once knew. Just days ago, my grandfather spoke on the phone, that low and raspy voice forever saved in my mind.

Just as soon as we lay him down, it seems, I'm bringing new life into the world. I feel that familiar surge in my body, a tightening, contractions coming in waves. I am breathing through a rippling pain that surges through me nonstop.

I step outside; trees tower and my husband holds my hand. My friend on the phone tells me she thinks it's time to go to the hospital. "I think I'm fine," I tell her. Because of the pandemic, I've been told I really can't go into the hospital until I'm ready to push that one, long primal push. "But, maybe you're right," I tell her, heaving through contractions.

When she arrives, she rubs my back, promising she will care for my older son when my husband and I head at last to the hospital. I go there to give birth to life in the midst of insurmountable death. A body tumbles like grace, right out of me, and I split my heart in two the minute my second son is born, lying on the bed, wrapped in wonder. *How in the world do we do this? How do we love in the midst of loss stacked upon loss?*

> We deliver life
> while disease
> makes *dear ones*
> disappear.

Here I am again, cradling life and death just like I did a few short years ago, and what I want more than anything else is to know why the man in the red tie lied. He stood there, right before us all, telling us through the television, again and again, that this all would go away, that it would disappear and we all would be fine.

On October 31, 2020, with lives being lost left and right to COVID-19, CNN published an interactive graphic highlighting the thirty-eight times that this man said the pandemic would "disappear."

"It's going to disappear. One day, it's like a miracle, it will disappear," he said on February 20, 2020, just shortly after the pandemic began.

"Because, you know, this virus is going to disappear. It's a question of when. Will it come back in a small way? Will it come back in a fairly large way? But we know how to deal with it now much better. You know, nobody knew anything about it, initially. Now we know we can put out fires," he said on May 6, 2020, with 26,722 average daily new cases in the United States.

"I'll be right eventually. I will be right eventually. You know I said, 'It's going to disappear.' I'll say it again. It's going to disappear, and I'll be right," he said on July 19, 2022, with 64,772 average daily new cases in the United States.[3]

He promised it would peter out, promised that even without a vaccine the virus would disappear, it'd just go away with everything going back to normal. No more death tolls recited on early morning newsreels, no more stories saturating radio stations. Like it'd all go away, as if it never even happened. Like it wasn't scary and frightening or like we didn't all feel the weight crushing down on our collective chest.

In times of death, in times of grave danger and downright degeneracy, what we need and want is to hear and know the truth about our lives—both what is good and what will inescapably grieve us.

What we need and deep down desperately want is to hear the truth from our leaders, our loved ones, and all those we do life with—the truth that there is no life without death. That it will come, unavoidably, in all the million ways this fractured world lets it come.

Comfort never
comes when we
lie about *loss*.

Tell us not that we are invincible but that death is inevitable. Remind us of the reckoning that is the reality of death. The nature of its loss, the way the color of flesh fades when blood fails to push through veins. The way the body cools and begins to decay. The way bones stiffen, still and lifeless.[4]

It's gut-wrenching and hard to think and talk about this. To wonder about it and weigh it against all we once thought to be true. To wonder where we go when we die, and whether or not we'll be aware of time or space or anything else in the afterlife, if we believe there really is one.

We can't hide in fear forever, though, from dialogues about death. Morticians and funeral directors are speaking up and writing articles and books, intent on demystifying the funeral industry and its systemic problems, as well as the history of death culture and death itself. Caitlin Doughty, for example, is a mortician, an advocate for funeral industry reform, and the bestselling author of *Smoke Gets in Your Eyes: And Other Lessons from the Crematory* as well as *From Here to Eternity: Traveling the World to Find the Good Death*. Of our cultural default to death, she writes:

> Looking mortality straight in the eye is no easy feat. To avoid the exercise, we choose to stay blindfolded, in the dark as to the realities of death and dying. But ignorance is not bliss, only a deeper kind of terror.[5]

This is the truth that surrounds us, but we do not want to hear, so we hide ourselves from death at all costs. Though it is everywhere, it's usually "veiled, or it's fiction,"[6] says Hayley Campbell, writer and author of *All the Living and the Dead: From Embalmers to Executioners, an Exploration of the People Who Have Made Death Their Life's Work*.

We have lost our proximity to death.

What would it matter to get it back?

What scares you about death and dying? Do you fear your own death? What are the worries that weigh you down?

It's the quintessential, quaint New England family that no one can quite get enough of—not enough of the sequels, the stage plays, the movies, the "more than 10 TV adaptations," the fan fiction, the Broadway musical.[7] We can't get enough of the millions of copies sold and its various translations, like *Kleine Frauen* and *Mujercitas*. And yet it's the story Louisa May Alcott didn't really want to write.

She wanted thriller and thunder; she wanted daring drama and darkness. She wasn't always known for that, however, even though her two books *Behind a Mask, or a Woman's Power* and *The Abbot's Ghost, or Maurice Treherne's Temptation* were both written (under the pen name A. M. Barnard) before *Little Women* was published. What she would eternally be known for is her endearing story about the March sisters: Meg, Jo, Beth, and Amy growing up in Massachusetts during the Civil War, among other tragedies. It soared, "selling the initial run of 2,000 books" within days of its 1868 release, and continues to endure in popularity entirely because of its matter. "Not a bit sensational," said Alcott. "But simple and true, for we really lived most of it."[8] Of this, Anne Boyd Rioux, author of *Meg, Jo, Beth, Amy: The Story of Little Women and Why It Still Matters*, writes:

> What seems like a tale from a simpler time turns out to be the product of a difficult and sometimes troubled life. What appears to be a sweet, light story of four girls growing up is also very much about how hard it was (and is) to come of age in a culture that prizes a woman's appearance over her substance. And what may seem an idealized portrait of an intact home and family is also the story of a family in danger of being torn apart.[9]

It's the "simple and true" part that resonates with Alcott's readers. It's getting lost inside the story of four sisters living and breathing through love and loss, reflecting back to readers all the grit and grief and goodness they know to be true of life. *Little Women* is also a sort of memorialization of America, capturing the country at a critical time in history: the raging and waging of the American Civil War, slavery, and the role of women.

Loss looms in *Little Women*, in the sense that it lingers not only in the lines of the book's pages but literally slips into the cracks in the floorboards and is welcomed between the walls of every room in Orchard House.

> The pleasantest room in the house was set apart for Beth, and in it was gathered everything that she most loved, flowers, pictures, her piano, the little worktable, and the beloved pussies. Father's best books found their way there, Mother's easy chair, Jo's desk, Amy's finest sketches, and every day Meg brought her babies on a loving pilgrimage, to make sunshine for Aunty Beth. John quietly set apart a little sum, that he might enjoy the pleasure of keeping the invalid supplied with the fruit she loved and longed for. . . .
>
> So the spring days came and went, the sky grew clearer, the earth greener, the flowers were up fairly early, and the birds came back in time to say goodbye to Beth, who, like a tired but trustful child, clung to the hands that had led her all her life, as Father and Mother guided her tenderly through the Valley of the Shadow, and gave her up to God.[10]

By no mistake, Beth dies in her beloved Orchard House. Propped up like a "household saint in its shrine"[11] she stayed rested in her room and cared for by her family, who were "forced to see the thin hands stretched out to them beseechingly"[12] until, finally, succumbing to complications from scarlet fever, she died.

Here, in *Little Women*, proximity to death is painfully close, depicting a time when death was welcomed in the home and preparing a body for burial was a "domestic task done by women."[13] The proximity to death is that, at once, it also offers a sacred kind of closeness that gives way to contemplative closure. After Beth dies, peace slips in through the walls of her room:

For the first time in many months the fire was out, Jo's place was empty, and the room was very still. But a bird sang blithely on a budding bough, close by, the snowdrops blossomed freshly at the window, and the spring sunshine streamed in like a benediction over the placid face upon the pillow, a face so full of painless peace that those who loved it best smiled through their tears, and thanked God that Beth was well at last.[14]

> Death was
> not always
> so distant.

What would it mean to you if proximity to death meant holding someone from being alone in their passing?

Industrialization, war, modernization, and advancements in technology always bring changes to the construct of society. Even the construct of family has undergone changes in even just the last century, as children have gone from working on family farms to going to school, "from being our employees to our bosses,"[15] writes Jennifer Senior, contributing editor for *New York* magazine and author of *All Joy and No Fun: The Paradox of Modern Parenthood.*

Children, once viewed as economical assets, are now investments. Parents no longer ask of their children, they pour into them, paying for top-notch education to ensure their children's success and, ultimately, theirs. With children no longer working or learning from home, all aspects of their livelihood have become outsourced. Their education now comes from professional teachers, their health is no longer attended to by house doctors but now comes from medical staff in private and public practices. Clothes are hardly ever made in the home, food is increasingly no longer made in the home, and burials are most certainly no longer held in the home.[16]

And while we have gained much from outsourcing these needs to alleviate the home from the burden of doing and being all, we have also lost much. Though industrialization brought helpful improvements and changes (like the advancement of trains, which made for easier transportation of bodies, resulting in the art of embalming: a way to preserve bodies for long train rides),[17] it also brought with it the eventual loss of literal and figurative proximity to death. Doughty shares:

> Before modern funeral homes, postmortem care was often as simple as washing and clothing the body before burial. No embalming, no mass-produced caskets, nothing the family couldn't do themselves. While some of these technologies have made it easier to care for the dead, they can also take agency away from families who otherwise tended to their sick and dying privately and intimately.[18]

Death stretched
long into lives,
lingered
not in coffins
but in rooms,
on beds, behind
compassionate
closed doors.

Death wasn't a task, it was a tending. Not a job to delegate but a joy to integrate the insistent care of a loved one into the fabric of a family. There was presence, proximity, and a preparedness with death. "[The March family] put away their grief," writes Alcott. "Each did his or her part toward making that last year a happy one."[19] Not that they denied the existence of their grief. Rather they lived through the expansiveness of it—finding a way to love through their loss, even still.

Have you ever had the honor of being with someone on hospice or palliative care, or in the season or moment of their passing? What was it like?

The fear we feel when we are faced with (or anticipating being faced with) death is real. It is not imaginary, not so easily vincible.

The fear is visceral, sending a shock that arrests all body and all thought. We really do freeze, immobile, our bodies falling into that "formal feeling," as Emily Dickinson writes about in her poem, "After great pain, a formal feeling comes—."[20]

In the face of death, we go still, cold, and archaic. Unfeeling, stiff. This is the shock of grief, as should be, for death threatens our notion of safety. Its presence, its proximity, and its inevitable, impending nature all paint a picture our brain interprets as dangerous. Death tells our brain and our body that in order to stay alive, we need to stay away and keep our distance.[21] This individual avoidance soon becomes a culture of collective avoidance, in which we shy away from death in our lives, work, classrooms, homes, and churches.

> The shock
> shows up
> to save you.

Death challenges everything, all the concepts and constructs of safety and security you and your brain have ever come to know and trust. It threatens your relationships with people, with places, with process. Grief is a conglomeration of agony and anxiety.

> The shock
> shows up
> to save you.
>
> But the shock
> cannot sustain
> you.
>
> It cannot
> carry you.
>
> **To live, we
> face the fear
> of death.**

A book I've come to deeply appreciate is *Superhero Grief*, edited by Jill A. Harrington and Robert A. Neimeyer. It explores loss and grief as experienced by our favorite comic book and on-screen superheroes, unshrouds the guise of their superhero strengths and courage, and pulls back the curtain on the conflict in their stories.

Grief is a conglomeration of agony and anxiety.

Exploring the many names and types of grief and loss, Jill first intends to let us know that the shock of death (or any loss) comes with a necessary task. "The first task," she writes, "for the bereaved is to recognize that the death is real." After the abrupt shock of death, the surprise that loss has in fact come our way, comes the time "to recognize, face, internalize the reality that death is real."[22]

> We perceive
> death, but we
> need also to
> process death.

Our bodies and brains want us to run and hide, forever in fear of this threat. It is like dining with Death when all we want is to avoid eye contact, avert attention, and ask for the check. Another date? *No, thank you.*

The shock shows up to save us, to protect us. To keep us alert in case we really are in a crisis of danger—a public shooting, a fire raging through nearby homes, blood loss from blunt trauma, infection in the body. But the shock cannot save you, cannot sustain you, cannot carry you forever.

> Bodies in crisis
> will collapse,
> will burn
> down.

If not now,
tomorrow
tomorrow
tomorrow.

After I gave birth to my second son, we took him to meet his pediatrician for the first time. We pulled a flower from our vase—a zinnia, if I remember correctly—and put it in a mason jar to bring to the doctor, a little sign of good hope in a hurting world.

She told us our son was fine, that everything about him was healthy and well. But also something else. "Your neck looks swollen," she told me. "Right there on the thyroid."

I am healthy. I am young. I drink my water. It can't be anything.

So when I find myself, months later, alone on a table in a small dark room getting a biopsy, that long thin needle stuck deep into the right side of my neck, I slip into shock:

I am young.
I am a mother,
I am needed.

Maybe
make me
immortal,
God?

They're testing for cancer, because the doctor tells me the lumps in my neck look malignant. The shapes are suspicious; there's a chance, though, that they might just be tumorous. And now everything within me is grasping for some sense of assurance. Can I imagine the future without me, imagine my two boys without a mother? *No. I am immortal. Have to be.*

I am entangled with the thought—no, the fear—of death. I imagine my husband shouldering the weight of my absence. I wonder if my death will hurt. Will I feel my lungs labor, will the skin on my bones surge and swell or burn with heat? If it's cancer and it kills me, will my mind stop racing before my heart stops beating? Or will I feel that too? Will I feel and sense life leaching, my spirit detached and partitioning, taken to dance with God?

Terror takes me toward death before a diagnosis does, and I am mourning what I have not yet lost. All those little losses—the missed birthday parties and graduations, the milestones, the growth charts on walls, the carpets stained with the footprints of small soles. I see the anniversaries I will never celebrate, gray peppered in and through the hair on my mother and father. My brothers standing over my grave and crying for me like I would for them.

If you could write a letter to Death, what would you say?

There is a unique kind of grief, anticipatory grief, which is experienced as the result of an expected or impending loss, like the kind you'd experience with a terminal cancer diagnosis.[23] Knowing that death is on the horizon but having time, little or large, between now and when it will happen opens sorrow, anger, guilt, emotional detachment, and social isolation.[24]

> The
> wait
> bears
> weight.

Anticipatory grief has two paths. On one path, the knowledge of an impending loss or death may be so overwhelming that it brings about feelings of guilt and powerlessness. Those preparing to depart from their loved ones may feel responsible for the pain they may cause in their wake. In certain situations, all variables based on individuals and individual circumstances, "anticipatory grief can trigger premature detachment."[25] The other path might allow someone the time and space to prepare for death and loss. Because it is expected, plans can be made in regard to possessions and other property. This may even give someone the chance to tie up loose ends, to bring reconciliation to relations.[26] Maybe, even if only in the smallest way, there is an opportunity for agency in anticipatory grief. Maybe, just maybe.

> The wait
> gives way
> to weigh
> the way
> you want *it*
> to be.

Sometime after we lost my grandfather to COVID-19, my mother told me that all of his affairs had been in order. Every debt paid, all clear—the car, the bills, everything in prime condition. My mother told me that it seemed he started preparing to pass about a year before he died, a year before he even contracted COVID-19. Maybe he knew his body was weakening, wilting. Maybe he, too, knew that feeling, that fear. Came face-to-face with the truth that he would not and could not be here forever.

I searched my memories for the messages my grandfather sent in that year before he died. Insistently asking me if I wanted the bike with the training wheels in his garage, the one he'd pulled off the side of the road from someone's unwanted belongings. In retrospect, I see that he was adamantly making sure he'd pass on cars or toys to each grandchild. Making the rounds, visiting all our different homes from New York to North Carolina. Giving us one last memory to carry us through the grief that would sure come.

On June 30, 2021, months after my grandfather's death and days after my biopsy, I wrote:

> They tell me there is a mass that is growing in my neck and that they will need to take three thin needles to it, need to test it, need to pull single cells from the swell of cells to tell me whether or

not it is cancer, whether or not the mass is making a mass mess of my body, my blood, my bones. Okay, I tell them. Okay to lay me down on that crinkling paper in the dark and cold room, okay to send me in alone, face hidden behind that layer of barrier and bad breath, okay to take thin needles to the thin of my neck, push and pull them hard and slow into the swell of cells while I lay there, looking at the life before my eyes, hearing the soundtrack of my sons, wondering about Time and whether it is a gift that's a curse, or if it's the other way around, or if I've altogether got it wrong, my finite frame trying to fathom the mind of God.

We wear mortality closer than our skin. **We are beginnings coming to an end**, and there is nothing beautiful about it. But there is life, that gift that comes before the grief, before the flesh fades and decays. Before breath expires, still and lifeless.

You can dread death all the livelong day. But, tell me—how will you spend your breath, your small breadth of life?

Spring will come
as spring will come.
But, first, that snowdrop,
coming with courage
through winter's
frozen floor.

———

For you,
pushing through
your fears of death,
a cold hard ground,
impenetrable but
by smallest seeds
of spring, soul's
hope.

———

Snow drops on bits
of earth like tears on cheeks
like ice on lakes like breath
immobilized in lungs
like the legacy of your life
forever *crystallized.*

Remember

- Tell us not that we are invincible.
- We can't hide in fear forever.
- To live, we face the fear of death.
- We are beginnings coming to an end.

Reflect

- What scares you about death and dying? Do you fear your own death? What are the worries that weigh you down?
- What would it mean to you if proximity to death meant holding someone from being alone in their passing?
- Have you ever had the honor of being with someone on hospice or palliative care, or in the season or moment of their passing? What was it like?
- If you could write a letter to Death, what would you say?

Respire

- Inhale: All my breath.
- Exhale: Is a gift.

Pansies, *Viola tricolor var. hortensis*
Meaning: You occupy my thoughts

PANSIES

for Faith

Never shall I forget those moments which murdered my
God and my soul and turned my dreams to dust.

Elie Wiesel, *Night*[1]

I can't recall the sound of a sanctuary, the bellowing of voices
reverberating reverent against sacred walls, falling upon sa-
cred floors. I can't recall the bright lights or the height of holy
stages. I tally the days since I've stepped foot into a church building,
and so far it is three years, three months, and counting.

I am not the same girl who, in my younger years, sat pious in
pews. Somewhere between that girl and me, and the twenty years
and six hundred miles that lie between, I have seen fire and I have
been burned. I have grown and I have groaned. Wars have been
waged and deaths have been mourned.

As of late, lives have been lost on gigantic, global scales. And
it turns out it isn't just me leaving my seat empty in the backs of
churches. "Black Americans feel under siege from the coronavirus
pandemic and raw from the police brutality," writes Dara T. Mathis
in her article "The Church's Black Exodus" in the *Atlantic*.[2]

She writes what I know, deep down in my bones, to be true. That this mass exodus is not a mere excuse and there is not some feel-good reason to sleep in on Sundays and keep from setting foot inside a church. Black parishioners and, honestly, others alike are not just leaving churches because of the pandemic and police brutality. We are all reeling from the reality of a layered, multifaceted pain.

Some are nursing another intimate wound: their church's failure to acknowledge their pain. Many Black parishioners, especially those at multiracial institutions, bristle when they hear rhetoric from church leaders that ignores how health inequities and racism are affecting the Black community. . . . The result is a quiet but resolute contingent of Black church members leaving their congregation to seek spiritual healing elsewhere.[3]

> We are weary
> and we are
> wary.
>
> *And*
> we are
> wary and we
> are weary.

I couldn't tell you the day it happened, couldn't tell you I kept it marked on my calendar, circled like an anniversary of sorts. *The day I left the church*, like some momentous moment. It was more like the tide—a gradual ebbing of ground, eroding relentless as the thrum of water and waves washed away my sure shore.

And I could prove to you that I still believe, could cross my heart and close my eyes. Hold my hands out in desperate, performative pleas until you see. I could cry louder and longer, jump higher and bleed prettier, until you see the charisma that we're all used to, characteristic of the age and of our ancestors, until you believe my faith is real. Until you know I, too, have that fire in my bones, that Word, combusting wild and all-consuming.

In the wake of a world wounded by a pandemic and protests, I wait, patiently counting the days, months, years. I wait to see what irreversible shifts that sickness and suffering will bring to the ways we do the things we believe we should do.

When you hear the word church, *what feelings, flashbacks, or fears come to you?*

There is a loss that comes by way of abandoning belief, or at least abandoning the customary practices constructed to uphold it. It taunts, invisible. Hides beneath layers of skin and bone, deep where the mind makes sense of moments and memory. It stands strong but, like stilts on sand, comes crashing down when wind and waves blow, a cruel catalyst of breath.

It is the tender unraveling, and sometimes traumatic tearing, of humanity's moral tapestry. Our sacred story of myth and meaning, of God and the garden, of the world and free will, of sin. It is the loss of faith, or religion, or piety, or whatever kind or forceful word you wish to call it.

In a 2021 *Charlotte Observer* article, my friend Rev. Kate Haynes Murphy wrote:

> The party line is to blame "this generation" for being less faithful, or "the media" for corrupting hearts or "the government" for taking prayer out of school. Once we've finished blaming those outside our communities, we turn to those inside and pressure them to give more, work more, sacrifice more to reverse the trend. But I don't think any of that is a faithful response. Because, while church membership is declining, people are still as hungry for the things of God as they ever have been. People are still seeking justice, forgiveness, hope, love and belonging. People are still desperate for mercy, for meaning, for second chances. People are still seeking the Holy, and the Holy One is still seeking people. So, the problem isn't with those outside the church, and it certainly

isn't with God. The problem—and it is a problem—is with us. The problem is that most of the church in America looks more like America than the body of Christ.[4]

Murphy's reference to "this generation" is an arrow that points to and pierces my own heart, because *it's me,* I am "this generation." It just might be you too. We are the ones still seeking justice, forgiveness, hope, love, and mercy, though not within the pews of a church. The ones desperate to know God and to make him known, though not from the glittering stage of a man-made sanctuary. We are the ones mucking up the many "terms of endearment." The non-verts, the exvangelicals, the deconstructors, the churchless, the godless, the irreligious, the faithless, the backsliders of our day.

The names all mix into one melting pot and, from the mouths of relentless churchgoers, are usually meant to cover the bases of all who keep distance from church buildings, productions, events, and even people. **In the chasm of all that is unsaid, there are miles of misunderstandings,** all interwoven with layers upon layers upon layers of loss. For many of us, myself included, it isn't a mere division, it's a death.

If you could speak out "all that remains unsaid" about your faith, what would you say?

There are words that resonate with the sting of this kind of loss, a story shared from within a greater narrative that bears witness to the kind of wound that comes from the loss of faith, or what looks like it. Elie Wiesel's story is that of a firsthand witness, watching children, women, and men suffer under the oppressive Nazi German concentration camps at Auschwitz and Buchenwald. Of suffering, faith in God, and death, this Nobel Peace Prize winner, Holocaust survivor, and author of *Night* writes:

Never shall I forget that night, the first night in camp, which has turned my life into one long night, seven times cursed and seven times sealed. Never shall I forget that smoke. Never shall I forget the little faces of the children, whose bodies I saw turned into wreaths of smoke beneath a silent blue sky. Never shall I forget those flames which consumed my faith forever. Never shall I forget that nocturnal silence which deprived me, for all eternity, of the desire to live. Never shall I forget those moments which murdered my God and my soul and turned my dreams to dust. Never shall I forget these things, even if I am condemned to live as long as God Himself. Never.[5]

We are disturbed if not destroyed by Wiesel's words, haunting and harrowing. He writes uniquely of his own experience, and yet it echoes with universal traumas and tensions and truths, his words vibrating with the visceral violence he experienced. Shared griefs carried by those who survived the same as he, as well as the rest of us who know what it is like to stare deep into the long, dark night—the black hole of loss, death, and pain from which our personal pains have commenced and were born.

Never shall I forget is all at once a vow of the inevitability of the involuntary: Wiesel's body will encode this chaos, make memory, forever marring the moment into his mind, saving the scenes in the very shivers down his spine. But also *Never shall I forget* is a voluntary vow. An unapologetic proclamation to read like a promise. *Never will I release this; ever will I remember the faces of innocent children, the bodies burning, the moments that murdered my God.*

At the mention of this, I might guess where your mind might find its way, assuming it is as cautious and curious as mine. *The moments that murdered my God*, as if God could be murdered. Is this blasphemous? No, not in the least bit. This phrase is not faithless at all. It is, in fact, the most faithful—and this is all the more strengthened by the following explanation:

In its form, this passage resembles two significant pieces of literature: Psalm 150, from the Bible, and French author Emile Zola's 1898 essay "J'accuse." Psalm 150, the final prayer in the book of Psalms, is an ecstatic celebration of God. Each line begins, "Hallelujah," or "Praise God." Here, Wiesel constructs an inverse version of that psalm, beginning each line with a negation—"Never"—that replaces the affirmative "Hallelujah" of the original. Whereas Psalm 150 praises God, this passage questions him. As such, both the form and content of this passage reflect the inversion of Eliezer's faith and the morality of the world around him. Everything he once believed has been turned upside down, in the same way that this passage's words invert both the form and content of Psalm 150.[6]

Wiesel's *Night* reads as if it could be the second book of Job or Psalm 151, lamenting on themes of suffering, loss, and falling away from faith in God. His lyrical passages are an honest lament, a releasing of searing sorrow. Yet Wiesel's words do more than just give witness to horror after horror; they give us a window into a way of walking through suffering with the magnitude of a moment that "murdered my God."

In an interview with Krista Tippett, host of the *On Being* podcast, Wiesel spoke into the common misconceptions that came after *Night* was published. "Never shall I forget those moments which murdered my God" has been largely misunderstood as Wiesel forsaking his faith. "I never divorced God," said Wiesel. Rather, it was his very belief in God that, Hebraically, beget his anger with God.[7]

> Within my traditions, you know, it is permitted to question God, even to take Him to task. . . . I sue God because in Hebrew, I bring him to rabbinic tribunal. And the arguments are all the arguments I take from the Bible and from his words. I mean, I take God's words and say, since You said these words, how is it possible that other things or certain things have happened?[8]

For Wiesel, and for others within his faith tradition, faith *is* taking God at his word, questioning him, even quarreling with him. Wiesel's faith in God never stopped. Though prayers were raised with rage and whys, prayers, nonetheless, never did cease to be raised.

We divert attention to our culturally conditioned worst fear, the words "murdered my God," so much so that we miss the evidence of Wiesel's achingly beautiful faith in God found in mere grammar. It lingers within the simple sentence structure, as seen through the possessive adjective *my* and the proper noun *God* it modifies.

> My God,
> *My God.*

God belongs to Wiesel, even after all. Even after the suffering, even after having "said these terrible words," he went on praying, went on with his faith in God.[9]

What comes to mind when you think of Wiesel's words, "Never shall I forget those moments which murdered my God"?

I want to whisper something to you that, in all the pious places you have pilgrimed, it's possible you might not yet have heard.

> **You are not**
> **a number.**

> Not a sum
> in a statistic.

> Not a penny
> in the offering
> plate.

> You are a life,
> preceded by the
> possessive
> grip of God.

My, you are
what comes
after *My*:

My child, he calls.
My child,
My child.

Don't let your eyes turn away from what burns and breaks before you, the racial tension and terror in the streets, the supremacy on stages, the insurmountable death tolls, the shootings in stores. Keep your eyes turned toward the ones suffering as you stand with them in solidarity, no longer satisfied with the comfort of a faith that can't shoulder the weight of a crumbling world—and its questions.

Keep your eyes turned toward the ones suffering.

Our world is inverted, turned upside down, just like the form of Wiesel's prayer. We go from praising God to questioning him, all the while losing faith. Let it look that way. Let it look and be however it needs to for however long it needs to. **Trust in that quiet work of faith**—which, by the way, isn't limited to being witnessed within the four walls of some brick building.

I want to know if you can sit with my pain, sit with my stench, sit with my stains. I want to know if you can make peace with the presence of pain-filled prayers whispered into the wind for nights without end. I want to know if you can crucify self-righteous anxiety, that impulse to induce salvation, and sit with someone in their silent suffering, their darkest night. Hear them. Hold them.

I want to know if you can hold space for however long it takes, for questions and grief, for suing God instead of explaining everything away with bullet points on PowerPoints.

Can you?

Pansies, for thoughts,
as you think about
all you've lost.

As you break,
as you bleed, all because
you believe.

———

Sit with me, disheveled under
the hard cold earth
in the dirt of dead things,
where the light of God
shines refracted,
dark with decay,
but illuminated, still.

———

Show me a sanctuary
that sits with the
suffering, doesn't hand
out healing in plastic bags,
returning home to warm bread
and bed, but suffers to stay,
to starve and stay starved.
Feel that eternal pang
of pain called love
for me, and we, and you.

Remember

- In the chasm of all that is unsaid, there are miles of misunderstandings.
- You are not a number.
- Trust in that quiet work of faith.
- I want to know if you can hold space for however long it takes.

Reflect

- When you hear the word *church*, what feelings, flash-backs, or fears come to you?
- If you could speak out "all that remains unsaid" about your faith, what would you say?
- What comes to mind when you think of Wiesel's words, "Never shall I forget those moments which murdered my God"?

Respire

- Inhale: Never shall I forget.
- Exhale: My God.

Part Two

IT MATTERS

REFLECTIONS *FOR* GRIEF

Passionflower, *Passiflora*
Meaning: Faith

PASSIONFLOWER
for the Cross

My God, my God, why have you forsaken me?

Matthew 27:46

I am on a plane flying to the desert, to the Casa, the Franciscan Renewal Center in Scottsdale, Arizona. I have never seen the desert, never seen cacti except for the little ones lined up for impulse buying in the checkout lines of grocery stores. I am one year out from giving birth to my second son, and I am heavy, burdened with the last two years of emotional baggage, plus one carry-on.

When I arrive at Phoenix Sky Harbor International Airport, as the plane taxis I am stunned and in awe, greeted by that majestic red mountain standing sacred against the beauty of a horizon, a landscape, new to my eyes.

When I get to the Casa, I am greeted by a desert garden. Surrounded by saguaro, I walk all slow-paced, kicking up dust and breathing in Arizona's air. Camera in hand, I contemplate the frames I want to capture, the memories I want to memorize, the beauty in this barren landscape set against a blue sky. I see something I've never seen before. Like a child's, my eyes are drawn to a grove of orange trees, vibrant and bright in someone's backyard. Birds are singing. *Birds sing here too? In the desert?* They jump along the dusty path decorated with miniature statues of Francis of Assisi.

The hot Arizona sun sinks warmth into my skin, and I feel something like weight unload from my being. I contemplate the last two years, what they've meant to me, meant to mother and writer me. I disentangle death in this desert. Trauma, my teacher, tells me where the tears have always been, as I look back. **I look out and breathe deep**, let my distress de-escalate.

> Inhale. Exhale.
>   Inhale. Exhale.
>   Inhale. Exhale.
>   Inhale. Exhale.
>   Inhale. Exhale.
>   Inhale. Exhale.

The expansive sky is grandiose without the glitter of green-leafed trees scattered about. I bask in this unborrowed space. Revel in this retreat, the remoteness of this place. Serenity soothes me, until *wow* something catches my eye. An impossibility?

No.

A paradox.

There, as if it'd been planted there on purpose, I see a bird's nest cradled in the thorns of a cactus. This saguaro—has it become a sacred holding of safe space for new life? Is the desert not as dangerous and desolate as I'd once deemed it to be? That nest is a significant sign of a place powerfully holding the dream of life amid all that's dry and dead and seemingly lost.

Have you ever been to a desert, sand dune, or barren landscape? How did the scenery move you to feel or think?

God of the Desert

> Then Moses led Israel from the Red Sea and they went into the Desert of Shur. For three days they traveled in the desert without finding water. When they came to Marah, they could not drink its water because it was bitter. (That is why the place is called Marah.) So the people grumbled against Moses, saying, "What are we to drink?" Then Moses cried out to the LORD, and the LORD showed him a piece of wood. He threw it into the water, and the water became fit to drink. (Exod. 15:22–25)

Who is this God of Israel? It is he who not only saves (Exod. 14) but also makes dead things come to life. Who is he that we might hear his Word, know its truth, and make it matter for our own deaths?

This we can know: the Israelites are a holy nation holding hope in God in one hand and fear in the other. They are a people who waver in their trust in God, hesitating to trust that he will sustain their bodies in miraculous ways they cannot do for themselves. Again and again, Israel falls into fear, thinking that the Lord has forsaken them and resolving to believe that their lack of abundance was caused by a lack of God's.

So, miracle after miracle, God moves: delivering the Israelites from slavery, parting the Red Sea, providing manna for food. God not only does the impossible but demonstrates to the Israelites that he is Immanuel: *God with us.* God guides Israel to see—it isn't the desert that endangers God's people. Rather, it is distance from God.

God of the desert invites us too. We are his people and, as such, he dares and invites us out into the places that bring us to dwell so closely with him that we can't help but be touched—transformed, even.

How has God moved in your life to keep you close to himself?

God in the Desert

> Then Jesus was led by the Spirit into the wilderness to be tempted
> by the devil. After fasting forty days and forty nights, he was hungry.
> (Matt. 4:1–2)

Just before Jesus is tempted in the desert wilderness, he is bap-
tized in the Jordan by his cousin John the Baptist (Matt. 3). There
he is affirmed in his identity and, soon after, begins his ministry. At
the start, Jesus is led by the Holy Spirit out into the desert, where
he fasts for forty days and forty nights. A desert experience, indeed.

> At once the Spirit sent him out into the wilderness, and he was
> in the wilderness forty days, being tempted by Satan. He was
> with the wild animals, and angels attended him. (Mark 1:12–13)

Satan tempts Jesus when he is without food and at his weakest.
Three times Jesus is tempted by Satan: to save himself, to provide
for himself, and to claim power for himself. Here, in this physical
desert, where wind whips at his face, sun scorches his skin, beasts
surround him, and food is denied him, Jesus is tested and tried.
And though physically he denies (and therefore lacks) that which
should keep him safe, secure, and sustained, we know this: "Jesus
was led by the Spirit into the wilderness." Though Jesus is in the
desert, God is with him. Immanuel: *God with us.*

This temptation is a foreshadowing of how Jesus will, in just a
few short years, hang on the cross as he finds himself in the midst
of another kind of desert.

There he is, metal nailed into the thin of his wrists from which
he hangs, the small bones bearing the weight of his whole body. He
bleeds from the back, blood painted across his bare skin, seeping
out from layers of cut flesh, every sigh a sting to the aching cells in
his body. Shoulders hang, fallen from their sockets, and his legs are
propped at an angle straining the muscles that move to help make
him breathe.[1]

Arms outstretched, he submits to the cruelest punishment and hangs before a crowd, hearing their jests hurled at him, heaved at him.

The rulers taunt him. *One:*

The people stood watching, and the rulers even sneered at him. They said, "He saved others; let him save himself if he is God's Messiah, the Chosen One." (Luke 23:35)

Then comes the temptation of the soldiers. *Two:*

The soldiers also came up and mocked him. They offered him wine vinegar and said, "If you are the king of the Jews, save yourself." (vv. 36–37)

Then one of the criminals bloodied on the cross beside Jesus. *Three:*

One of the criminals who hung there hurled insults at him: "Aren't you the Messiah? Save yourself and us!" (v. 39)

Jesus, tormented, hangs on the cross and hears an echo of the three temptations that taunted him in the desert. He has all power to bring himself down, all reason to save himself, all power and reason to prove that he is, in fact, the King of the Jews.

Instead, he endures the jeering crowd, remains suspended with arms outstretched, and dies a desolate death—saving not himself but all the world. He hangs human, memories of his life flashing before his eyes. He hangs holy, eternal love holding him to that cross. He hangs, water filling his body, breath labored, lungs filling, blood spilling, heart pressure dropping, thirst holding.[2]

He hangs,
dying.

Jesus takes upon his shoulders every sin of the world. Then he utters all he can muster up, the only words that can display the depth of the pain he feels. *"My God, my God, why have you forsaken me?"* he cries (Matt. 27:46), reciting Psalm 22, the ancient words instilled deep within his soul. Of every lash, of every whip, every sneer, every nail, every ribbon of flesh torn, and every other torture he has endured . . . what summons these words most is not his physical suffering but that of his spirit—distance from his Father.

> My God,
> my God,
> why have you
> forsaken me?
> abandoned me?
> *deserted* me?

What do you think distance from the Father might feel like? Scary? Hopeless? Empty? Lonely? Unfathomable?

In his sermon "Lama Sabachthani?" Charles Spurgeon wrote:

It was no fancy, or delirium of mind, caused by his weakness of body, the heat of the fever, the depression of his spirit, or the near approach of death. He was clear of mind even to this last. He bore up under pain, loss of blood, scorn, thirst, and desolation; making no complaint of the cross, the nails, and the scoffing. We read not in the Gospels of anything more than the natural cry of weakness, "I thirst." All the tortures of his body he endured in silence; but when it came to being forsaken of God, then his great heart burst out into its "Lama sabach-thani?" His one moan is concerning his God. It is not, "Why has Peter forsaken me? Why has Judas betrayed me?" These were sharp griefs, but this is the sharpest. This stroke has cut him to the quick: "My God, my God, why hast thou forsaken me?" It was no phantom of the gloom; it was a real absence which he mourned.[3]

Jesus takes on the weight of all sin and sickness and suffering, and he carries with it the wages deserved: death—separation from God. Jesus, who has never known separation from the Father, who relies on the Father for all things, who has been infinitely found in fellowship with the Father* and eternally tethered as one with the Trinity,† is deserted by the Father because of the sin on his shoulders.

> Jesus lays down his life.
> Crucified, lets death come close
> for the sake of reconciling all,
> to come close to God.

**Jesus's greatest grief
brings our greatest gift** —   life, and

life with God.

In Arizona, in blazing heat on a February day, I make my way up a mountain with the group. Water bottles are full, cameras are loaded, phones are ready. We begin, together, all of us stepping in stride one after another. As we climb higher and higher, my heart beats loud and the whole landscape before me appears like a mirage. I realize my sick body is not as strong as it once was.

Newly adapting to medication, I'm learning the way of this new, broken body. It cannot carry me as far as I thought it could or should. There once was a time when making this hike would have been possible, like the time I hiked in Panama and ascended

---

* "No one has ever seen God, but the one and only Son, who is himself God and is in closest relationship with the Father, has made him known" (John 1:18).

† "In the beginning was the Word, and the Word was with God, and the Word was God. He was with God in the beginning. Through him all things were made; without him nothing was made that has been made" (vv. 1–3).

a trail with gear on my back. But here, in this moment, I cannot. I separate from my group and descend to find a rock to sit on and take a pause.

Looking out over the bluff, elevated high above the ground with a beautiful sky in the background, I feel the metaphor make its way into my heart: I see and sense the desertion of the desert. Yet my soul is finding a filling, a kind I haven't experienced in the last few years. Here, in the desert, abandoned and in seclusion, I am finding rest. With nothing offered to me but barrenness I am filled to the brim, finding that God is speaking loudly in the silence of this solitary place.

He is the fullness of the brush, the holy sweeping in the wind, the sweet water in a dry and thirsty land.

My heart and mind are brought to ponder deeply on the paradox. Can I—will I— look through a lens that lends itself to see life in all my desert places? I feel a seed of truth take root in my heart like a promise, like God touching his finger to the most tender place in my heart. *He is with me,* like flowers pushing through the ground in a desert bloom. He is the fullness of the brush, the holy sweeping in the wind, the sweet water in a dry and thirsty land.

In barrenness,
we can still be
filled to the brim.

———

The desert and the parched land will be glad;
    the wilderness will rejoice and blossom.
Like the crocus, it will burst into bloom;
    it will rejoice greatly and shout for joy. (Isa. 35:1–2)

Jesus took on cosmic distance with God so that we might know closeness with God. On the cross, he took on the spiritual desert of death so that we might have eternal fellowship with God. *My God, my God,* he cried. And also, *My God, my God,* he recited, repeating Scripture even in his greatest grief. Like Wiesel writes in *Night,* "Never shall I forget those moments which murdered my God," Jesus clings through the greatest horror, still calling on God, still claiming him.

> One for me,
> and one for you,
> and one for we, and thee, and all
> his blood spilled out, so red and true
> a love for me and some for you
> blooming out, his passion bright
> in that hour before the night
> a passionflower, for we,
> for all, and thee, our Lord.
> The King of all.

———

> The parched mouth
> makes melodies *and*
> sings the sweetest songs
> of deliverance
> from death
> manna from the heavens
> makes our mourning turn to
> d e s e r t dancing

———

That you would
cross that cosmic chasm
for *us,* make light of
night and space—
your gravity grabs,
takes our scattered stars
and holds them
magnified
all matter made
close by your force
of love.

Remember

- Look out and breathe deep.
- Jesus's greatest grief brings our greatest gift.
- Jesus took on cosmic distance with God so that we might know closeness with God.

Reflect

- Have you ever been to a desert, sand dune, or barren landscape? How did the scenery move you to feel or think?
- How has God moved in your life to keep you close to himself?
- What do you think distance from the Father might feel like? Scary? Hopeless? Empty? Lonely? Unfathomable?

Respire

- Inhale: My God, my God.
- Exhale: You have not forsaken me.

Ivy, *Hedera*
Meaning: Attachment

IVY

for the Burial

Jesus said to her, "Woman, why are you weeping? Whom are you seeking?"

John 20:15 ESV

We walk the long white corridor at the North Carolina Museum of Art. It echoes with the sound of footsteps, families lost in wonder just like we are. We are captivated by the art—the classical Roman sculptures all magnificently made of marble, and those passionate bronze bodies, "The Thinker" and "The Kiss," so distinctly Auguste Rodin.

The museum is busy and bustling, not at all a sleepy Saturday morning. People walk with their children hand in hand, while strollers are rolled in and through the myriad of entryways that open to ancient and contemporary collections of art. Of all that is so beautifully stunning and powerfully moving, I am really only there to come face-to-face, for the first time, with that tortured artist soul. *Vincent van Gogh.*

I have never seen a painting of his, though I've always wanted to. His wavy strokes. His melancholic swirls of sorrow. The evocative emotion and the pain in his paint palette. I am there for van Gogh and nothing much else. That is, until I round this one corner in the long white corridor. I turn and right there, hanging on the wall in all its humble glory, is the most captivating painting, framed by four equal edges of wood stained deep. Beneath the painting is a label. It reads:

Willem van Aelst
Dutch, 1626–1683
Vanitas Flower Still Life
Circa 1656–1657
Oil on canvas

Purchased with funds from
the State of North Carolina, 1952 (52.9.57)

This finely detailed but impossible bouquet includes flowers that bloom at different times during the year, transforming it into a convincing illusion to those in the know. Van Aelst makes each flower seem to come alive, but this realism should not distract the viewer from the work's underlying message of vanitas.

Vanitas, the temporary nature of earthly things, is emphasized through the presence of dying flowers, partially eaten leaves, insects, and the mouse eating a seed. Our brief time on earth, symbolized by the crystal watch with a blue ribbon, passes as quickly as the beauty of each bloom.[1]

I see the sheen and the strokes, the canvas textured and telling me of its age. I see a bouquet of flowers blooming to life with stunning vibrancy, its pops of color against a muted background. My children tug on my shirt and strangers walk past me, their footsteps echoing loud in the acoustics of the gallery. None of this matters to me at the moment, though. I am enraptured, as I should be. For I am utterly transported, my mind traveling back to 1656. Or was it 1657, when van Aelst took oil and canvas and painted this piece that now takes my breath away?

I cannot take my thoughts off this painting, cannot begin to fathom why this word *vanitas* strikes such a chord deep in my heart. I want to know why the museum label says that this painting is a "convincing illusion to those in the know."[2] In the know of what?

Does this impossible bouquet project some pretense of perfection? Does it allude to an illusion that hides the truth about life . . . about death?

When I leave the museum, I resolve myself to research. I return to visit the museum reference library to learn all about vanitas paintings. I learn about the transcendence of this theme of life and death, how it rose in popularity during the Renaissance but has origins that can be traced all the way back to ancient Egypt.[3] I learn about the intentional symbolism of earthly possessions, like watches and silver serving ware, juxtaposed against items from the natural world like flora and fauna.[4] I learn about the joys of everyday life pitted against the inevitable natural ending of all things—all of these things coming together in vanitas paintings in order to create a scene "to remind viewers of their own eventual death."[5] A reminder intended to encourage its viewers to "uphold their integrity in this world before meeting the harsh judgment of their divine maker in the next."[6]

There it is—there is the tug on my heart that van Aelst's "Vanitas Flower Still Life" touches. Looking at this painting, I feel it in my bones. Life offers no illusion, no pretense of impossible bouquets. The truth and the fact is *yes*, life is as beautiful as a bouquet of blooming flowers—but it is also fleeting. Van Aelst's impossible bouquet would better paint a picture of truth had it flowers blooming to life and arranged beside other flowers wilting away.

For life and death will always go hand in hand. The flowers will eventually fall, the fruit will eventually decay. And *we* will die—we will someday decay.

> The promise in our
> blood   '
>
>   '
>
>   '
>
>   '
>
> all bodies will bend
> and bow at last *b r e a t h.*

There is a pang, the faint echo of pain at this truth. And I want to know, Is there anything else about these paintings that, perhaps, speaks more of life than death and decay? Something that paints a picture of life *even in the midst of loss?*

Then I remember the secret of the natural world—the silent story that science screams for the ones who have eyes to see it, for the ones laid low, eyes locked on the mystery. There is one deep truth that can be distilled from vanitas paintings that put death and decay on display. It is the fact that *"death makes life possible."*[7] It's the miracle of the microbial world, the work of fungi and mushrooms, their purpose the process that makes life possible in all living things— from beasts and bogs to human bodies.[8]

Could it be that death has something to say about life?

What would it matter to ponder this?

> *What feelings or thoughts rise to the surface when you think about the symbolism of flowers, watches, clocks, and elements of decay in vanitas paintings?*

God of the Garden

> Thinking he was the gardener, she said, "Sir, if you have carried him away, tell me where you have put him, and I will get him." (John 20:15)

In Jesus's day, the ritual of burial and caring for the ones you loved and lost looked like preparing their body with oils and wrapping it in clean linen, then letting the body lay within a tomb for up to one year. During this time, the flesh would decompose, leaving only the bones. Thus, after that year of decomposition, the remains would be gathered and placed into an ossuary, a box made specifically to hold bones. This box would then be stored forever in a designated spot within the family's tomb.[9]

This is not the case with Jesus, though. Here, in John 20, in an account following Jesus's crucifixion and burial, we have Mary, a devout follower—one who'd cried in the corners of crowds at his crucifixion. She encounters Jesus—face-to-face—his body unbroken, lungs breathing, and all.

> But Mary was standing outside the tomb, weeping; so as she wept, she stooped to look into the tomb; and she saw two angels in white sitting, one at the head and one at the feet, where the body of Jesus had been lying. And they said to her, "Woman, why are you weeping?" She said to them, "Because they have taken away my Lord, and I do not know where they put Him." When she had said this, she turned around and saw Jesus standing there, and yet she did not know that it was Jesus. Jesus said to her, "Woman, why are you weeping? Whom are you seeking?" Thinking that He was the gardener, she said to Him, "Sir, if you have carried Him away, tell me where you put Him, and I will take Him away." Jesus said to her, "Mary!" She turned and said to Him in Hebrew, "Rabboni!" (which means, Teacher). (vv. 11–16 NASB)

When Mary visits Jesus's tomb, her grief only grows at the realization that not only has she lost someone she loves but now his body is lost too. *His body lost?* How would she care for and take care of all that should remain—his body and then his bones? Frantically, she cries, "Tell me where you've put him, and I will take him away!"

"I will take him away," says Mary. She will, as the original Greek reads, *airō*—raise up, elevate, lift up—his body.[10] This weeping woman declares that, in her own strength, she will lift Jesus's body, as simply as one lifts a stone from the ground. *Tell me where you've put him, and I will take him away*—as if she could carry Jesus in his death.

Tell me where you've put him, and I will take him away—as if there would ever be a tomb strong enough to box in the bones of Jesus. As if he could be kept in the ground, in the grave.

> Mary, don't you know—
>
> He is not laid up in
> the ground, his bones,
> above earth, they
> are not in the grave.

He is alive, lungs
breathing, he is well,
this walking garden—
this God of the
ground.

Mary doesn't know. And yet, somehow, she gets it right. Knee-deep in grief, she doesn't recognize Jesus at first. *Why should she?* The last she saw her beloved savior, he was bruised and bloodied. *How would she recognize his now resurrected body?* Mary happens upon this man she thinks is the gardener. And, in fact, her thinking isn't far from the truth. Standing before her is not only her resurrected Rabboni but the God of the Garden—the maker and keeper of things teeming with life, things that grow from and through the ground.

"Why are you crying?" he asks, prying and pressing into her in-grained grief. Then **he calls her by name**. *Mary,* he says. She didn't recognize his resurrected body but she recognizes his voice—still the same kind voice she remembers of her savior. She hears the truth in his tone. That she hasn't lost his body or lost him. She cannot grieve over that which is not gone, cannot raise up, elevate, lift up that which has already been raised.

She cannot lift up the one who, alone, lifts all things to life. For, though Jesus is standing with her then and there, he also stood before the beginning of time when the world cracked open—light pouring from the sky, dust heaving into the lungs of humankind, life teeming over all the terrain.

What ideas, images, memories, or Scriptures come to mind when you think of God as a gardener?

God in the Garden

Now the LORD God had planted a garden in the east, in Eden; and there he put the man he had formed. (Gen. 2:8)

God, of all things in the world, creates a garden—a lush land teeming with layers of life. By his Word, he creates all living things— all seed-bearing trees, all birds of the air, all beasts of the earth, every mountain, every mushroom, every microscopic microorganism. And all is good and well and works just as it should, until the man and the woman give in to that push of darkness, draped in the devil's disguise. They take that one bite into the forbidden fruit, and their eyes become opened, death entering through the devil's door.

> Death is the
> *devil's demise,*
> death is the
> *devil's design.*

Death slips in. *Like a sweep of wind, a draft undetected under the door.* This is how and when God's good garden gets polluted and planted over with the seed of death.

But God is not merely the gardener *of* the garden. He is God *in* the garden, walking among the garden. God steps and stoops low into the place where sin and shame have sprouted up like weeds.

> Then the man and his wife heard the sound of the LORD God as he was walking in the garden in the cool of the day, and they hid from the LORD God among the trees of the garden. But the LORD God called to the man, "Where are you?" He answered, "I heard you in the garden, and I was afraid because I was naked; so I hid." (Gen. 3:8–10)

God stands with the man and the woman, not merely in his good garden but in their sin. He walks among them, walks toward them, even in the aftermath of their downfall. Even so, this death was not his design. **God's plan was for life, not distance or destruction or disease or death.** But gardener God has a green thumb. He knows just what his creation needs to thrive and survive.

He grounds his hand in the garden, deeply touching and tending to it. To rescue his garden from the grip of death, he plunges—not only to death but beyond it. God, sending his beloved Son to this thorn-torn world, doesn't just give Jesus over to death but designs it so that Jesus conquers death—is raised to life *after* death.

> Christ comes—
> he lives, he dies.
>
> The propitiation
> purposed to bring
> perpetuation—his
> death makes life
> possible.

His resurrection embodies the miracle of the microbial world—the hidden work of fungi that feed off death. His is the death that *makes life possible*.[11] He takes what seems only to be a display of death and wrings life from it, mirroring the miraculous work of mushrooms (which are *his* creation) and making death part of a process that perpetuates life.[12] Though death was not the dream, through God's design life can come from and through death.

> Jesus *wrings* life
> from death, Jesus
> *rewrites* death.

Behold, this man in the garden, this risen savior. *Rabboni*, Mary says, whispering into the wind. The teacher is still teaching, still tending to his followers with the truth that death cannot keep those who believe. **Death cannot hold those buried with Christ.**
Just as he has said, and just as he has done.

> *Ivy*, you are the garden's immortal grip,
> always reaching, always teaching
> with your vines to intertwine
> when other blooms and stems retire,
>
> *still*
> you cling and climb.

———

In the dark pit of earth,
black and bleak,
cold and cruel,
there, invisible to eyes,
hides the mystery of life—
a seed, buried unassuming—
a plant of green in
a plot of ground to
bring about new life.

Remember

- He calls her by name.
- God's plan was for life, not distance or destruction or disease or death.
- Death cannot hold those buried with Christ.

Reflect

- What feelings or thoughts rise to the surface when you think about the symbolism of flowers, watches, clocks, and elements of decay in vanitas paintings?
- What ideas, images, memories, or Scriptures come to mind when you think of God as a gardener?

Respire

- Inhale: He came to die.
- Exhale: That I might live.

Lily of the Valley, *Convallaria*
Meaning: Return of happiness

LILY OF THE VALLEY
for New Life

Ought not the Christ to have suffered these things and to enter into His glory?

Luke 24:26 NKJV

Science says the moon makes earth's tides swell. It says the two—earth and moon—are tethered to one another through gravitational force, and all of earth's oceans rage when the moon waxes full and strong.

When I stand at my grandfather's grave for the first time in the two years since his burial, I stand there under a waxing moon and in the swell of my own oceans undulating under the hold of grief's gravity. There I am, between the trees, standing in the chill of an arctic air mass with no scarf, no hat. I want to move my mouth and make words come from my lips, but I cannot, with my face frozen in New York's cold, bitter wind.

A pile of bones I am, shivering and shaking, putting off all I want to say to my grandfather, laid low beneath the ground. Can I really whisper confessions aloud into the wind, telling him how it feels like he, just days ago, slipped his way through the back door of my townhome? It feels like just yesterday he walked up my stairs and sang a song or two to his mesmerized great-grandson. I want to look long and loving, one last time, into his face; I want to memorize the constellation of freckles on his cheeks and smooth that furrow in his brow. I want to tell him not to worry, that I'm okay, we're all okay. And then I'd cry somewhere where he wouldn't see me, so my tears don't hold him back from earth's release.

In so many ways, I'm still that young girl from all those years ago, standing at my grandmother's casket, grief pulling still. Swelling and surging, like a gaping hole in the center of me, grasping for what always evades and eludes.

In all I've grieved, I've yet to learn to let go of every little loss. But I have learned about what it looks like to deeply love and live even still. Maybe that's what matters. Maybe we're not meant to escape grief's grip.

Grief undulates. It moves, unnamed, unknown.

A fleeting thing that is, for better or worse, forever here to stay.

I feel you,
though you're far away.
Grief's gravity
keeps us tethered, always.
Memory wanes,
faint and still.
Memory waxes,
floods and swells.
I reach for you, extend
lengthy limbs in search of you.
The hole you filled
rounds larger
still.

Science says *how* the moon makes earth's tides swell, but my soul wants to know *why.* Why does the pale moon tug at earth's oceans, making a tidal of waves that rise and fall in perpetual cycle? Who set the celestial globe in orbital dance with earth?

And why does grief come the way it comes? Why does it stay the way it stays, tangled and tethered to the soul, always inseparable? Where is the good in grief's gravity?

How do you think the moon's phases relate to grief?

God of the Heavens

> In the beginning God created the heavens and the earth. Now the earth was formless and empty, darkness was over the surface of the deep, and the Spirit of God was hovering over the waters. (Gen. 1:1–2)

In the beginning, the world cracks open with light pouring from the sky. The heavens and the earth are set into motion and begin their orbital pathway, their purpose. Land divides sea from shining sea, trees sway and dance, seeds spread and sprout. All animals awaken at the sound of Creator's voice. He breathes, dust heaving into the lungs of the first humans, and in his good time the earth tilts formed and full.

And Jesus is right there for and through it all, stringing the stars and breathing life into both man and animal. For "the Word was with God, and the Word was God" (John 1:1). He is in all, through all, for all, before all.

> He is God of the galaxy,
> God of the heavens,
> God of all.

When Jonah, in fear, flees the Lord's call and heads for Tarshish, he seeks safety on a ship and falls asleep on the lower deck. The seas rage with a storm, threatening the ship and all who are on it. The captain finds Jonah asleep and says, "How can you sleep? Get up and call on your god!" (Jon. 1:6). Then the sailors join in, casting lots and demanding to know whose fortune and fault have brought upon them this violent, raging storm. "Where do you come from?" they ask him. "From what people are you?" (v. 8). Jonah confesses, "I am a Hebrew and I worship the LORD, the God of heaven, who made the sea and the dry land" (v. 9).

It means everything to note this—and it means everything to *know* this, deeply know it in the heart. When Jonah utters these words to the sailors who, not long before, were afraid of the raging storm and had each cried out to his own god (v. 5), he is, by way of admission, declaring that the God of heaven is "no mere tribal deity, but the true God who had created the very heavens."[1]

These sailors do not simply hear the word, they come to believe it. The raging sea surrounding them gives proof that Jonah's God—so obviously in control of the raging sea—is *the* God. God of heaven, God of sea, God of all.

> Then they took Jonah and threw him overboard, and the raging sea grew calm. At this the men greatly feared the LORD, and they offered a sacrifice to the LORD and made vows to him. (Jon. 1:15–16)

By this name, this declaration, God is distinguished and distinctly set apart. He is no mere man-made image or idol. He is the Maker of all, Creator of all. He is all-knowing and all-powerful. Therefore, he is to be feared and followed. Worshiped and revered. All are to be in awe of him and obey. This Lord is lord of all—the one, true God of heaven.

And still, God is so much more and does so much more than speak forth life and summon light. He does more than suspend planets and tend to trees. God is more than power and holiness and might. God is mercy; all love and compassion are cradled within his hands. God is father and friend; he is intimately involved in all our intricacies.

He is not merely God of the heavens; **he is the God who comes close**. He is the God who stands in the stench of humanity's sin, who stretches his arms out on the cross, plunging all people to light and life. He is the God who dies and rises to life again, not simply just to save us but to be with us. He is the God who conquers death and comes to life, intent on being with us one last time before ascending *into* the heavens.

> Why is it that God
> who rules and resides
> over the heavens. Who
> is resurrected and raised
> to the heavens, comes to
> the people of earth. Cares
> for the people of earth.
>
> Why is it that?

When you think of God creating the heavens, what images, words, Scriptures, paintings, or songs come to mind?

God in the Heavens

Now that same day two of them were going to a village called Emmaus, about seven miles from Jerusalem. They were talking with each other about everything that had happened. As they talked and discussed these things with each other, Jesus himself came up and walked along with them; but they were kept from recognizing him. (Luke 24:13–16)

Jesus is gone and nothing but grief remains. *Imagine it.* Imagine the death or disappearance of someone you've let your life revolve around. Imagine they are gone and you cannot get them back; imagine the ripple of losses that would inevitably ensue and unfold. Imagine a severance in the gravitational pull between two celestial bodies that had been tethered together in time and space.

If the earth ever lost its moon, the ocean's tides would more than rage.

Seasons would shift.
Newly hatched turtles would wander adrift without moonlight.
Earth's tides would shrink in size.
Animals reliant on the tides would no longer survive.
Ecosystems would go awry.[2]

Earth, its gravity broken, would grope and groan, its littlest losses bringing about even the greatest grief.

So, then, imagine the missing Messiah. Imagine the hope of Israel buried in a hole . . . and then his body is *gone*. Imagine the confusion and the shock—the sorrow and sense of loss—of the disciples reeling in the new reality of Jesus *gone*.

On the same day Mary comes face-to-face with the resurrected Jesus, she runs to tell the other disciples she has seen Jesus—that he's alive. But the disciples don't believe her or any of the other women who come to profess the same. *How could they?* Just days before the disciples had seen, with their own eyes, Jesus crucified and buried. Still, in his desperation, Peter checks Jesus's tomb to see if these women could somehow be right.

Peter, however, got up and ran to the tomb. Bending over, he saw the strips of linen lying by themselves, and he went away, wondering to himself what had happened. (v. 12)

The disciples are already dealing with Jesus's death—already dealing with the loss of their closest friend, the loss of their teacher and his teachings, the loss of that dream for kingdom come. And now there's a rippling of rumors that Jesus's body is gone too. For this, they taste a deep, great grief.

On the same day of this rumored resurrection, two of the disciples take a walk and head for the village of Emmaus. They are reeling, reminiscing over the last few days. *Jesus is gone. The women have claimed that Jesus is alive. His body is missing.* All the little ways in which their lives have been upended.

On the way to Emmaus, a man comes alongside and walks with them. "What are you discussing together as you walk along?" the man asks. This man is Jesus. He is resurrected and unrecognizable. The disciples stand there with their faces "downcast," says the Word, and ask this man (Jesus) how it is that he knows nothing of what they are talking about. Then they proceed to tell him every sorrow in their souls, everything they know and feel and fear, as they walk along together.

> "About Jesus of Nazareth," they replied. "He was a prophet, powerful in word and deed before God and all the people. The chief priests and our rulers handed him over to be sentenced to death, and they crucified him; but we had hoped that he was the one who was going to redeem Israel. And what is more, it is the third day since all this took place. In addition, some of our women amazed us. They went to the tomb early this morning but didn't find his body. They came and told us that they had seen a vision of angels, who said he was alive. Then some of our companions went to the tomb and found it just as the women had said, but they did not see Jesus." (vv. 19–24)

Without even realizing it, they confess every little loss and greatest grief to Jesus, their teacher and closest friend. And also without realizing it, they confess they still don't see it all, still don't understand or believe that Jesus had done all he said he would do—including being raised back up to life. "We had hoped that he was the one who was going to redeem Israel," they say. They can't see beyond their grief, though Jesus is in their grasp, right there in their midst.

Later that evening, as they approach Emmaus, the disciples stop for the night and invite the man to stay with them. Together, at the table, the man breaks bread and gives thanks. It is at this moment they finally recognize the man—*it's Jesus.*

> He *is* risen.
> He *is* alive.

Then Jesus disappears. At once they return to Jerusalem and tell the other disciples—as well as all those assembled with them—that *it's true.* The women are right. Jesus has risen, and he is alive. He has done just what he said he would do but also, very simply, *he is here, walking with us and among us* once again.

Jesus, the Word who was with God and is God himself, is not merely raised to a new life but also raised to his relationships. Resurrected, he returns to the people and places that once knew and held him. In this, the resurrection is not only powerful because Jesus fulfilled what was prophesied but also it becomes a deep display of intimate, relentless love. The resurrection positions Jesus to step into the gap of grief experienced by the very ones he knew and loved.

> While they were still talking about this, Jesus himself stood among them and said to them, "Peace be with you." They were startled and frightened, thinking they saw a ghost. He said to them, "Why are you troubled, and why do doubts rise in your minds? Look at my hands and my feet. It is I myself! Touch me and see; a ghost does not have flesh and bones, as you see I have." (vv. 36–39)

Jesus, in his resurrected body, presents himself to prove the prophecies about him are all *yes.* But also Jesus, in his resurrected body, presents himself to lavish love on his friends in the midst of their loss. "Look at my hands and feet," he says. "Touch me and see." He's not gone and not a ghost. Neither is he distant and uninvolved in the life, love, livelihood, and losses of the ones he loves.

He is there, in the flesh, fulfilling the prophecies of old but also filling his friends up with promises to carry them into their tomorrows. He is there, in the midst of their pain, not merely to present solutions to their problems but to simply be present.

He is like the moon, eternally strung in the sky and tethered to earth—the gravitational force of his unfathomable pull on us, both unstoppable and inseverable. For "neither death nor life . . . neither height nor depth, nor anything else in all creation, will be able to separate us from the love of God that is in Christ Jesus our Lord" (Rom. 8:38–39).

> He is not merely the God of the heavens.
> He is, deeply, the God who comes close to man.
> His is the death that makes life possible.
> Could it be that his is the love that makes loss livable?

Yes, it's true, Jesus is on a mission for the whole world, and he makes the men and women he knows his missionaries. "Touch me and see," he tells them. And then they tell—they tell, they tell, they tell. But also he's saying, "Touch me and see. See and let it soothe you. Believe that I am here. I am with you, even in this." For the God of heaven has a habit of making himself present in the midst of people's pain. **He cannot help but meet us where we are.**

> He, in all *hereness*,
> gathers with the ones
> he loves. He greets
> them in their grief
> before going on
> to glory, to
> *heaven.*

When he had led them out to the vicinity of Bethany, he lifted up his hands and blessed them. While he was blessing them, he left them and was taken up into heaven. Then they worshiped him and returned to Jerusalem with great joy. And they stayed continually at the temple, praising God. (Luke 24:50–53)

As Jesus ascends into heaven, he bestows a blessing over his disciples, words to carry them into the days ahead—words to recall and return to. Then they worship him and return to Jerusalem with great joy. Yes, they return, with joy, to the place that holds memories of their greatest grief—the city of Jesus's crucifixion. The location where they once lost it all.

Of the disciples' response to worship, Pieter G. R. de Villiers writes in his article "The Resurrection as Christ's Entry into His Glory,"

> They not only become witnesses of the word as a result of the transformative experience of the resurrection, but they become worshippers of Jesus as the One in whom God acted and remained with them in times of alienation and stress.[3]

It's true. The power and passion of God is not only that he is God *of* but God *in*. It is his hereness that holds us, his closeness that compels us. It is his presence and proximity that put his passion on display, ever pulling us in and drawing us close to his heart.

When Jesus ascended into his glory, into *heaven*—it was not before he remained *here* on earth, blessing his closest friends in the middle of their brokenness.

If Jesus were to bless you in the middle of your brokenness, what would you want him to say?

As long as I live, I will never again touch the hands of my grandfather, never again hear the cackle of my grandmother's laugh. I will walk out the rest of my brief time on this earth wanting them and missing them. Needing them but not having them. I will always fear losing what I haven't yet lost. The world will take and take, and my heart will always wring out trauma's tears, cried and spilled out, ever mourning the way life breaks and betrays and borrows without returning that which should belong.

And *you*.

There are those things you will never unsee, unhear, undo, or understand. Your life will thrash with the gravity of grief, its waves rising and falling in and through the seasons. Little losses, and your fear of them, will loom. They will stand unknown and unseen by others. Demanding attention but falling dim into the background.

Sometimes the dreams will fade and bodies will fail. Some days fear will fill as futures fall away, further still.

And, you know the holidays will hollow holes inoperable into that holding heart of yours. Every cycle of the sun, every Christmas on the calendar, every empty chair at the Easter table, every birthday with no candles to blow.

> Sorrow will
> swell and surge
> and sting and
> stay. Like the
> moon, ever
> present, often
> hidden in the
> light of day.

But there is this—the truth of the fact that **God is with you in your grief**, giving space for sorrow, welcoming you as you slowly find your way. *He greets you in your grief before going on to glory, to heaven.* He waits with you as you grope and groan for words that give language to loss—all those little and large. He stops and he stoops, lays low, right there with you in the suspension of all things. He blesses you even in your brokenness, even as you beg for kingdom come. For new earth, new world.

I want to be the one to tell you that *this* is why your little losses, the whole sweep of your griefs, matter. **Little losses are longings that look like God's heart.** They point to the places in us that ache for what has been lost, and they ache when the world isn't as it should be, could be.

We grieve not only the absence of these lost things but also in the mere presence of pain. I couldn't tell you to put that away any more than I could tell the moon to sever its tie with earth.

I can, however, bestow a *blessing*. Words I'll leave to lead you as you feel grief, fight grief, fear grief. One day we will all ascend like Christ into heaven—to that place with no pandemics, no pain, no

shootings, no sorrows. No tragedies, no tears, no disease, no death.
For now, though, let there be heaven on earth.
    Let there be God of heaven over us.
    Let there be God of heaven with us.
    Amen.

> Your grief
> gives glimpse
> to God. So, may you never
> lose the lament of your
> *little losses.*
>
> May you not despise
> them, for
> they are proof
> that pain wasn't
> a part of
> God's
> plan.

> ———

> Let us be led by
> *the lily of the valley*
> its fragrance like
> a bell to ring the
> sweetest song,
> calling us home
> toward heaven, home
> with heaven, sweet sighs
> bringing sorrow to reprieve.

> ———

> He is not there,
> not his body and
> not his bones.

He lives,
body erected,
life resurrected
in your heart, and
in heaven's
h o m e.

Remember

- He is the God who comes close.
- He cannot help but meet us where we are.
- God is with you in your grief.
- Little losses are longings that look like God's heart.

Reflect

- How do you think the moon's phases relate to grief?
- When you think of God creating the heavens, what images, words, Scriptures, paintings, or songs come to mind?
- If Jesus were to bless you in the middle of your brokenness, what would you want him to say?

Respire

- Inhale: God comes to me.
- Exhale: God cares for me.

RESOURCES
for Reflection

FLOWERS FROM RACHEL

ACKNOWLEDGMENTS

Thank you is an
understatement,
a blanket of words that
beg for replacement.

Shin, until death do us part. This book, both the living out and the writing of it, would not be possible without you. Yours in Limbo, forever.

Milo Mountain and Aaro Sky, you are love in a world of loss.

Mom and Dad, Umma and Appa, Grandma, and Uncle Bubbles, I hope you know: you are living examples of how to live and love through loss.

Mia, I love you and I cannot lose you. Forget-me-not, dearest friend.

To all my family: may gardens ever bloom where we grieve.

To the friends who hold my roses, thorns and all: Rebecca, K.J., Courtney, Meredith, Kayla, Angel, Katie, Sarah, Jazmine, Tiffany, Liv, and Lamar.

To my team at Revell Books: it's a joy to bring light and love into the world with you.

Special thanks to my beta readers for braving my book before it was ready. Your suggestions and stories were like candles lighting the way for me: Candyce Gauthier, Susan Arvieux, Donna Godsell,

233

Eunice Ho, Valerie Slaybaugh, Ruth Point, Judy Ports, Cindy M. Chen, Kayla-Rhae Johnson, Kristine Karen-Lynn Amundrud, Alison Simpson, Katherine Nadene, Shay Carter, Drew Dixon, Neidy Hess, Sarah E. Koch, Mia Arrington, Katie Drobina, Kristin Vanderlip, and Jazmine Lampley.

Isaiah 60:20

A MESSAGE FROM RACHEL

Dear you,

It sort of feels like a eulogy, coming up with words to end our time together. I have all good things to say, of healing and of hope. Of release and remembrance. I wonder—is it the same for you?

Our time together doesn't have to end here, though. We can keep the pages turning, the thoughts rolling, the tears welling, the hearts healing, and the love rising. We can take what we started and see it through its groaning and growing. Best of all, we can do it together.

It's my hope that the discussion questions in this book serve as candles on your quest, helping to light the path as you find your way through grief and loss. Return to these questions. Run with them, rage with them. Reckon, always, with the fact that it all matters.

I hope to hear your story sometime. Find me at RachelMarie Kang.com to connect and keep in touch.

All,

Rachel Marie Kang

READING GROUP GUIDE

What is the hardest loss or situation you've ever survived? What is the hardest loss or situation you've ever seen someone else survive?

If you could build a fence to keep your loved ones close, where would you build your fence, and who would you keep inside?

If you returned to your homeland or hometown, what would you do? Where would you go?

Who is the first friend you made? Why was this friend special or significant to you?

Where do you think dreams come from, and what purpose do they serve? What is one dream you will never give up on?

How have you experienced the loss of innocence? Who in your life has fulfilled the role of M'Baku, guiding you to process pain?

In life, we may not always encounter the cures we need or want. Nevertheless, we can still take care of our bodies. How are you learning to do just that?

Is there an unnamed loss that you wish had a name? What is the loss, and what would you name it?

If you could sit down for coffee with your younger self, what would you say? What advice would you give for growing older?

How do we sustain the minor with the major? How do we hold grief and joy together?

What healing and hope have you found in community?

If you could have one wish granted in the hour of your passing, what would you wish for?

What enchants, or first enchanted, you to believe in God?

What have you learned from this book? How have you come to see that your losses—little and large—matter?

FOR FURTHER READING

Grief Books

A Faith That Will Not Fail: 10 Practices to Build Up Your Faith When Your World Is Falling Apart by Michele Cushatt

A Grief Observed by C. S. Lewis

A Hole in the World: Finding Hope in Rituals of Grief and Healing by Amanda Held Opelt

Superhero Grief: The Transformative Power of Loss by Jill A. Harrington and Robert A. Neimeyer, eds.

What Cannot Be Lost: How Jesus Holds Us Together When Life Is Falling Apart by Melissa Zaldivar

Spiritual Growth Books

Even If Not: Living, Loving, and Learning in the in Between by Kaitlyn E. Bouchillon

In Want + Plenty: Waking Up to God's Provision in a Land of Longing by Meredith McDaniel

Native: Identity, Belonging, and Rediscovering God by Kaitlin B. Curtice

Peace Is a Practice: An Invitation to Breathe Deep and Find a New Rhythm for Life by Morgan Harper Nichols

The Best of You: Break Free from Painful Patterns, Mend Your Past, and Discover Your True Self in God by Alison Cook

The Lord Is My Courage: Stepping through the Shadows of Fear toward the Voice of Love by K. J. Ramsey

To Light Their Way: A Collection of Prayers and Liturgies for Parents by Kayla Craig

Funeral Books

All the Living and the Dead: From Embalmers to Executioners, an Exploration of the People Who Have Made Death Their Life's Work by Hayley Campbell

How We Die: Reflections on Life's Final Chapter by Sherwin B. Nuland

Smoke Gets in Your Eyes: And Other Lessons from the Crematory by Caitlin Doughty

Creativity Books

Create Anyway: The Joy of Pursuing Creativity in the Margins of Motherhood by Ashlee Gadd

Let There Be Art: The Pleasure and Purpose of Unleashing the Creativity within You by Rachel Marie Kang

On Reading Well: Finding the Good Life through Great Books by Karen Swallow Prior

The Irrational Season: The Crosswicks Journals, Book 3 by Madeleine L'Engle

Fiction

Firekeeper's Daughter by Angeline Boulley

Hamlet by William Shakespeare

Hotel Oscar Mike Echo by Linda MacKillop

Ophelia by Lisa Klein

Children's Books

Chasing God's Glory by Dorina Lazo Gilmore-Young
Fly High: Understanding Grief with God's Help by Michelle Medlock Adams and Janet K. Johnson
In My Heart: A Book of Feelings by Jo Witek
The Rabbit Listened by Cori Doerrfeld

Journaling Books

Breathing through Grief: A Devotional Journal for Seasons of Loss by Dorina Lazo Gilmore-Young
Rest: A Journal for Lament by Kristin Vanderlip
Stuff I'd Only Tell God: A Guided Journal of Courageous Honesty, Obsessive Truth-Telling, and Beautifully Ruthless Self-Discovery by Jennifer Dukes Lee

Companion Books

Floriography: An Illustrated Guide to the Victorian Language of Flowers by Jessica Roux
The Book of Common Courage: Prayers and Poems to Find Strength in Small Moments by K. J. Ramsey
When Change Finds You: 31 Assurances to Settle Your Heart When Life Stirs You Up by Kristen Strong

Memoirs

Crying in H Mart: A Memoir by Michelle Zauner
Night by Elie Wiesel
Notes on Grief by Chimamanda Ngozi Adichie
Tell Me the Dream Again: Reflections on Family, Ethnicity, and the Sacred Work of Belonging by Tasha Jun
The Year of Magical Thinking by Joan Didion

NOTES

Author's Note

1. Clarissa Pinkola Estés, *Women Who Run with the Wolves: Myths and Stories of the Wild Woman Archetype* (New York: Ballantine Books, 1995), 15.

2. Karen Swallow Prior, *On Reading Well: Finding the Good Life through Great Books* (Grand Rapids: Brazos, 2022), 15.

3. Rachel Marie Kang, *Let There Be Art: The Pleasure and Purpose of Unleashing the Creativity within You* (Grand Rapids: Revell, 2022), 94–95.

4. Amy Ansalone, "History of Funeral Flowers," 1-800-Flowers.com, accessed February 19, 2023, https://www.1800flowers.com/blog/flower-facts/history-of-funeral-flowers/.

5. Jessica Roux, *Floriography: An Illustrated Guide to the Victorian Language of Flowers* (Kansas City: Andrews McMeel Publishing, 2020), ix.

Visitation

1. William Shakespeare, *Hamlet* (New York: Penguin, 1998), 15.

2. Joan Didion, *The Year of Magical Thinking* (New York: Alfred A. Knopf, 2005), 3.

3. Shakespeare, *Hamlet*, 15.

Chapter 1 Marigold for Grace

1. J. K. Rowling, *Harry Potter and the Order of the Phoenix* (New York: Warner Bros., 2003), 824.

2. As quoted in Frederick Woolverton, "Are We Born into Trauma?," *Psychology Today*, September 15, 2011, https://www.psychologytoday.com/us/blog/the-trauma-addiction-connection/201109/are-we-born-trauma.

3. Jill Bergman, "Skin-to-Skin Contact?," La Leche League International, accessed February 19, 2023, https://www.llli.org/skin-to-skin-contact.

4. Alison Cook, *The Best of You: Break Free from Painful Patterns, Mend Your Past, and Discover Your True Self in God* (Nashville: Nelson Books, 2022), 22–23.

5. Tzvi Hersh Weinreb, "Survivors of Trauma," *Jewish Herald-Voice*, accessed February 19, 2023, https://jhvonline.com/survivors-of-trauma-p25011-220.htm.

6. J. K. Rowling, *Harry Potter and the Deathly Hallows* (New York: Warner Bros., 2007), 321.

7. Rowling, *Harry Potter and the Deathly Hallows*, 328–29.

8. Justin McCurry, "'To My Last Breath': Survivors Fight for Memory of Hiroshima and Nagasaki," *Guardian*, accessed February 19, 2023, https://www.theguardian.com/world/2020/aug/06/to-my-last-breath-survivors-fight-for-memory-of-hiroshima-and-nagasaki.

9. McCurry, "'To My Last Breath.'"

10. Rowling, *Harry Potter and the Order of the Phoenix*, 824.

Chapter 2 Daffodil for Love

1. August Wilson, *Fences* (New York: Penguin, 1986), 61.

2. Jane Anderson, "The Impact of Family Structure on the Health of Children: Effects of Divorce," *Linacre Q* 81, no. 4 (November 2014): 378–87, https://www.ncbi.nlm.nih.gov/pmc/articles/PMC4240051/.

3. Jill A. Harrington and Robert A. Neimeyer, eds., *Superhero Grief: The Transformative Power of Loss* (New York: Routledge, 2021), 60.

4. Wilson, *Fences*, xii.

5. Wilson, *Fences*, 77.

6. Wilson, *Fences*, 96–97.

7. Wilson, *Fences*, 90.

Chapter 3 Camellia for Home

1. Michelle Zauner, *Crying in H Mart: A Memoir* (New York: Alfred A. Knopf, 2021), 10.

2. "Katrina Babies Official Trailer HBO," YouTube video, 2:53, uploaded by HBO, August 15, 2022, https://www.youtube.com/watch?v=NjteP4qBqn4&t=173s.

3. Radheyan Simonpillai, "'I Didn't Understand My Trauma': How Hurricane Katrina Marked New Orleans' Young," *Guardian*, accessed February 19, 2023, https://www.theguardian.com/tv-and-radio/2022/aug/22/katrina-babies-documentary-edward-buckles-new-orleans.

4. Edward Buckles Jr., "Katrina Babies: Discussion Guide, 2022," HBO, accessed February 19, 2023, https://www.hbo.com/movies/katrina-babies.

5. Eric Hemenway, "Native Nations Face the Loss of Land and Traditions," National Park Service, accessed February 19, 2023, https://www.nps.gov/articles/negotiating-identity.htm.

6. Julia G. Young, "The Situation at the U.S.-Mexico Border Can't Be 'Solved' without Acknowledging Its Origins," *Time*, March 31, 2021, https://time.com/5951532/migration-factors/.

7. Julia G. Young, "A Wall Can't Solve America's Addiction to Undocumented Immigration," *Washington Post*, accessed January 9, 2019, https://www.washingtonpost.com/outlook/2019/01/09/how-americans-became-addicted-undocumented-immigration/.

8. Cook, *Best of You*, 22–23.

9. Harrington and Neimeyer, *Superhero Grief*, 72.

10. Zauner, *Crying in H Mart*, 10–11.

11. Kang, *Let There Be Art*, 106.

12. Jerry M. Burger, "What If Your Home Were Suddenly Gone?," *Psychology Today*, May 10, 2011, https://www.psychologytoday.com/us/blog/returning-home/201105/what-if-your-home-were-suddenly-gone.

13. Roni Beth Tower, "The Meaning of 'Home,'" *Psychology Today*, November 4, 2021, https://www.psychologytoday.com/us/blog/life-refracted/202111/the-meaning-home.

14. Kang, *Let There Be Art*, 104.

15. Marsha A. Stoltz, "'Unprecedented Blessing': 285-Year-Old Land Use Deed Returned to Ramapough by Sloat Family," *North Jersey*, June 4, 2022, https://www.northjersey.com/story/news/bergen/mahwah/2022/06/04/ramapough-land-use-deed-returned-sloat-family-ramapo-college/7500057001/.

16. "The Ramapough Lunaape of New Jersey," Our Land, Our Stories, accessed February 19, 2023, https://our-land-our-stories.libraries.rutgers.edu/exhibits/show/olos-history/the-ramapough-lunaape-of-new-j.

17. "An Indian Canoe, Perhaps 1,000 Years Old, Unearthed by Dredge in Witteck Lake, N.J.," *New York Times*, December 20, 1923, https://www.nytimes.com/1923/12/20/archives/an-indian-canoe-perhaps-1000-years-old-unearthed-by-dredge-in.html.

Chapter 4 Forget-Me-Not for Friendship

1. L. M. Montgomery, *Anne of Green Gables* (New York: Simon & Schuster, 2014), 226.

2. Harrington and Neimeyer, *Superhero Grief*, 60.

3. Montgomery, *Anne of Green Gables*, 84.

4. Kang, *Let There Be Art*, 163.

5. Kira M. Newman, "Why Your Friends Are More Important Than You Think," *Greater Good Magazine*, July 7, 2020, https://greatergood.berkeley.edu/article/item/why_your_friends_are_more_important_than_you_think.

6. Prior, *On Reading Well*, 140.

7. Montgomery, *Anne of Green Gables*, 226.

Chapter 5 Edelweiss for Dreams

1. Angeline Boulley, *Firekeeper's Daughter* (New York: Henry Holt, 2021), 14.

2. Boulley, *Firekeeper's Daughter*, 11.

3. Donald Miller, *Through Painted Deserts: Light, God, and Beauty on the Open Road*, abridged audiobook, narrated by Donald Miller (Audible, 2007), 09:50.

4. Adapted from Rachel Marie Kang (@rachelmariekang), "I studied writing in the same small town where my grandfather was murdered," Instagram, December 13, 2019, https://www.instagram.com/p/B6AyhbqFTZq/?igshid=Y2IzZGU1MTFhOQ==.

Chapter 6 Daisy for Innocence

1. *Black Panther: Wakanda Forever*, directed by Ryan Coogler (Burbank, CA: Marvel Studios, 2022), Disney Plus, 1:41:55.

2. Joan Didion, "Goodbye to All That," in *Slouching towards Bethlehem* (New York: Farrar, Straus & Giroux, 1968), 225–38. This essay is one of my favorite pieces

of writing. It personally resonates with me, and it also famously encapsulates the disillusionment that many of New York City's residents and admirers come to feel about their beloved city . . . and themselves.

3. Estés, *Women Who Run with the Wolves*, 161.

4. *Wiktionary*, s.v. "innocent," accessed February 19, 2023, https://en.wiktionary.org/wiki/innocent#Etymology.

5. Lauren Frias, "Paintings by Ukrainian Children Depict Horrors of War and Dreams of the Future in Bright, Colorful Illustrations," *Insider*, January 16, 2023, https://www.insider.com/children-displaced-ukraine-war-capture-scenes-of-conflict-in-art-2023-1.

6. Pia Krishnankutty, "'Will Never Forget the Sound of Bodies Smashing on Ground'—9/11 Survivor, 19 Years Later," *The Print*, September 11, 2020, https://theprint.in/features/will-never-forget-the-sound-of-bodies-smashing-on-ground-9-11-survivor-19-years-later/500339/.

7. "Victims of Sexual Violence: Statistics," RAINN, accessed February 19, 2023, https://www.rainn.org/statistics/victims-sexual-violence.

8. "UNICEF in Ukraine," UNICEF USA, accessed February 19, 2023, https://www.unicefusa.org/mission/emergencies/child-refugees-and-migrants/war-ukraine.

9. Cierra Chenier, "The 'Katrina Babies' Are All Grown Up and We Have Something to Say," *Essence*, August 24, 2022, https://www.essence.com/culture/katrina-babies-are-all-grown-up/.

10. Mark Hughes, "Review: Breathtaking 'Black Panther: Wakanda Forever' Will Top $1 Billion Box Office," *Forbes*, November 11, 2022, https://www.forbes.com/sites/markhughes/2022/11/11/review-breathtaking-black-panther-wakanda-forever-will-top-1-billion-box-office/?sh=6fa16d4e6b77.

11. *Black Panther: Wakanda Forever*, 00:26:05.

12. *Black Panther: Wakanda Forever*, 1:41:55.

13. Amy F. Davis Abdallah, "Embracing Ritual on Your Journey through Grief," Redbud Writers Guild, June 1, 2021, https://redbudwritersguild.com/embracing-ritual-on-your-journey-through-grief/.

14. Didion, *Year of Magical Thinking*, 3.

Chapter 7 Chamomile for Calm

1. *Iron Man*, directed by Jon Favreau (Burbank, CA: Marvel Studios, 2008), Disney Plus, 00:38:18.

2. Kang, *Let There Be Art*, 128.

3. Harrington and Neimeyer, *Superhero Grief*, 55.

4. National Geographic (@natgeo), "Can we 'cure' aging? Scientists are racing to crack the code," Instagram, December 29, 2022, https://www.instagram.com/p/CmxJBXCvJ3F/?utm_source=ig_web_copy_link&igshid=MzRlODBiNWFlZA==.

5. Fran Smith, "Can Aging Be Cured? Scientists Are Giving It a Try," *National Geographic*, December 28, 2022, https://www.nationalgeographic.com/magazine/article/aging-cure-longevity-science-technology-feature.

6. Madeleine L'Engle, *The Irrational Season: The Crosswicks Journals, Book 3* (New York: Crosswicks, 1977), 16.

7. Walt Whitman, "Song of Myself, 51," Poets.org, accessed February 19, 2023, https://poets.org/poem/song-myself-51.

8. Jazmin Tolliver, "'Iron Man' Makes History as the First MCU Movie Inducted into National Film Registry," Yahoo! News, December 15, 2022, https://news.yahoo.com/iron-man-makes-history-first-191731961.html.

9. Rachel Marie Kang, "How to Hold Your Bones," *Mothering Spirit*, September 28, 2022, https://motheringspirit.com/2022/09/how-to-hold-your-bones/. Reprinted by permission.

Chapter 8 Carnation for Vilomah

1. *Pieces of a Woman*, directed by Kornél Mundruczó, written by Kata Wéber (Burnaby: BRON Studios, 2021), Netflix, 00:05:10.

2. Harrington and Neimeyer, *Superhero Grief*, 72.

3. Jae Ran Kim, "Ambiguous Loss Haunts Foster and Adopted Children," North American Council on Adoptable Children, February 9, 2009, https://nacac.org/resource/ambiguous-loss-foster-and-adopted-children/.

4. Suzanne Phillips, "The Loss of a Child to Suicide: Complicated Pain," *Psych-Central* (blog), January 13, 2014, https://psychcentral.com/blog/healing-together/2014/01/the-loss-of-a-child-to-suicide-complicated-pain#1.

5. Alan D. Wolfelt, "Helping SIDS Survivors Heal," PsychCentral, accessed February 19, 2023, https://griefwords.com/index.cgi?action=page&page=articles%2Fhelping19.html&site_id=2.

6. Stephen Moeller, "The Grief of a Miscarriage," *The Grief Recovery Method* (blog), September 27, 2017, https://www.griefrecoverymethod.com/blog/2017/09/grief-miscarriage.

7. Leow Wen Pin, "Understanding Their Grief: 5 Ways to Support Parents of Children with Special Needs," Salt&Light, March 8, 2022, https://saltandlight.sg/service/5-ways-to-support-parents-of-children-with-special-needs/.

8. Karla Holloway, "A Name for a Parent Whose Child Has Died," *Duke Today*, May 26, 2009, https://today.duke.edu/2009/05/holloway_oped.html.

9. Holloway, "A Name for a Parent."

10. Richard Brody, "'Pieces of a Woman,' Reviewed: A Tale of Grief Gets Lost in the Details," *The New Yorker*, January 12, 2021, https://www.newyorker.com/culture/the-front-row/pieces-of-a-woman-reviewed-a-tale-of-grief-gets-lost-in-the-details.

11. *Pieces of a Woman*, 00:05:10.

12. March of Dimes, "Infant Mortality. These Two Words Should Never Go Together," March of Dimes, September 21, 2022, https://www.marchofdimes.org/find-support/blog/infant-mortality-these-two-words-should-never-go-together.

13. Mary C. Lamia, "The Silent, Post-Abortion Grief of Men," *Psychology Today*, September 30, 2022, https://www.psychologytoday.com/us/blog/intense-emotions-and-strong-feelings/202209/the-silent-post-abortion-grief-men.

14. Child Welfare Information Gateway, "The Impact of Adoption," Child Welfare Factsheets for Families, accessed February 19, 2023, https://www.childwelfare.gov/pubs/factsheets-families-adoptionimpact/.

15. Kylie Agllias, "'You're Dead to Me:' Why Estrangement Hurts So Much," *Psychology Today*, October 3, 2014, https://www.psychologytoday.com/us/blog/family-conflict/201410/you-re-dead-me-why-estrangement-hurts-so-much-0.

16. Danielle Campoamor, "People Who Have Had a Miscarriage Say One Taylor Swift Song Has a Powerful Meaning for Them," TODAY, October 21, 2022, https://www.today.com/parents/pregnancy/taylor-swift-song-miscarriage-bigger-than-the-whole-sky-rcna53433.

Chapter 9 Baby's Breath for Matrescence

1. Lisa Klein, *Ophelia* (New York: Bloomsbury, 2006), 241.

2. "A Baby Grizzly's Story," *Growing Up Animal*, season 1, episode 1, directed by James Hemming, Melanie Gerry, and Nick Smith-Baker (Burbank, CA: Disney Plus, 2021).

3. "A Baby Grizzly's Story."

4. "A Baby Grizzly's Story."

5. Alexandra Sacks, "The Birth of a Mother," *New York Times*, May 8, 2017, https://www.nytimes.com/2017/05/08/well/family/the-birth-of-a-mother.html.

6. Klein, *Ophelia*, 102, 116.

7. Klein, *Ophelia*, 3.

8. Klein, *Ophelia*, 302.

9. Erin Zimmerman, "The Identity Transformation of Becoming a Mom," *The Cut* (blog), May 25, 2018, https://www.thecut.com/2018/05/the-identity-transformation-of-becoming-a-mom.html.

10. Zimmerman, "Identity Transformation of Becoming a Mom."

11. Sacks, "Birth of a Mother."

12. Rachel Marie Kang (@rachelmariekang), "It occurred to me late last evening, as the Carolina sun slipped into hiding," Instagram, May 19, 2019, https://www.instagram.com/p/BxpKvTfFNVe/?igshid=Y2IzZGU1MTFhOQ==.

13. L'Engle, *Irrational Season*, 16.

14. Rachel Marie Kang, "I Wear Stains More Than I Wear Smiles," *Coffee + Crumbs* (blog), May 31, 2023, https://www.coffeeandcrumbs.net/blog/2023/5/29/i-wear-stains-more-than-i-wear-smiles.

Chapter 10 Azalea for Suicide

1. *Seven Pounds*, directed by Gabriele Muccino, written by Grant Nieporte (Culver City, CA: Columbia Pictures, 2008), Netflix, 0:01:00.

2. Suicide Prevention Resource Center, "Means of Suicide," Suicide Prevention Resource Center, accessed February 19, 2023, https://www.sprc.org/scope/means-suicide.

3. Patrice Harley, "People Who Die by Suicide with a Firearm Are Less Likely to Have Sought Treatment," Rutgers University, March 14, 2022, https://www.rutgers.edu/news/people-who-die-suicide-firearm-are-less-likely-have-sought-treatment.

4. Harley, "People Who Die by Suicide with a Firearm."

5. *Seven Pounds*, 0:01:00.

6. Austin Eamnarangkool, "The Crisis by Ennio Morricone," Medium, December 10, 2017, https://medium.com/@austinalbyauralaesthetics/the-crisis-by-ennio-morricone-f5c2d842cb5.

7. Rachel Marie Kang (@rachelmariekang), "I remember those water shoes," Instagram, March 8, 2019, https://www.instagram.com/p/Buw66JkFKfC/?igshid =Y2IzZGU1MTFhOQ==.

Chapter 11 Hyssop for Plagues

1. Thomas Nashe, "A Litany in Time of Plague," Poets.org, accessed February 19, 2023, https://poets.org/poem/litany-time-plague.

2. Didion, *Year of Magical Thinking*, 3.

3. Harrington and Neimeyer, *Superhero Grief*, 81.

4. Laura Parker, "Rare Video Shows Elephants 'Mourning' Matriarch's Death," *National Geographic*, August 31, 2016, https://www.nationalgeographic.com/animals /article/elephants-mourning-video-animal-grief.

5. Barry Yeoman, "When Animals Grieve," National Wildlife Federation, January 30, 2018, https://www.nwf.org/Home/Magazines/National-Wildlife/2018/Feb -Mar/Animals/When-Animals-Grieve.

6. Alfie Shaw, "Painted Wolf Singing Ritual Filmed for First Time," BBC Earth, accessed May 25, 2023, https://www.bbcearth.com/news/painted-wolf-singing -ritual-filmed-for-first-time.

7. Shaw, "Painted Wolf Singing Ritual Filmed."

8. Corinne Ofgang and Erik Ofgang, "More Than 250,000 Are Dead. Why Is There So Little Collective Grief?," Elemental, December 2, 2020, https://elemental .medium.com/more-than-250-000-are-dead-why-is-there-so-little-collective-grief -dd33c547ca09.

9. Jason Vermes, "Collectively, We're Grieving Far More Than COVID-19 Deaths, Say Experts," CBC Radio, February 21, 2021, https://www.cbc.ca/radio/checkup /how-are-you-coping-during-the-pandemic-1.5919233/collectively-we-re-grieving -far-more-than-covid-19-deaths-say-experts-1.5921879.

10. Diya Chacko and Sam Schulz, "Coronavirus Today: Where's America's Shared Grief?" *Los Angeles Times*, May 22, 2020, https://www.latimes.com/science/news letter/2020-05-22/grief-churches-nursing-homes-coronavirus-today.

11. Shakespeare, *Hamlet*, 31.

12. William Shakespeare, *Romeo and Juliet* (New York: Simon & Schuster, 2011), 159.

13. Nashe, "Litany in Time of Plague."

14. Steve Mentz, "Poetry for a Time of Plague," Stanford Humanities Center, accessed February 19, 2023, https://shc.stanford.edu/arcade/interventions/poetry -time-plague.

15. Mentz, "Poetry for a Time of Plague."

16. 9/11 Memorial & Museum, "Solidarity after 9/11," 9/11 Memorial & Museum, accessed February 19, 2023, https://www.911memorial.org/learn/resources/911 -primer/module-4-solidarity-after-911.

Chapter 12 Snowdrop for Death

1. Louisa May Alcott, *Little Women* (London: Penguin Classics, 1989), 375.

2. Kang, *Let There Be Art*, 173.

3. Daniel Wolfe and Daniel Dale, "'It's Going to Disappear': A Timeline of Trump's Claims That Covid-19 Will Vanish," CNN, October 31, 2020, https://www.cnn.com/interactive/2020/10/politics/covid-disappearing-trump-comment-tracker/.

4. Moheb Costandi, "What Happens to Our Bodies after We Die," BBC, May 8, 2015, https://www.bbc.com/future/article/20150508-what-happens-after-we-die.

5. Caitlin Doughty, *Smoke Gets in Your Eyes: And Other Lessons from the Crematory* (New York: Norton, 2014), ix.

6. As quoted in Albert Samaha, "Here Are the Nitty-Gritty Details of Death Nobody Wants to Talk About," *New York Times*, August 17, 2022, https://www.nytimes.com/2022/08/16/books/review/all-the-living-and-the-dead-hayley-campbell.html.

7. Amaranta Sbardella, "Before Writing 'Little Women,' Louisa May Alcott Penned 'Blood and Thunder,'" *National Geographic*, December 3, 2021, https://www.nationalgeographic.co.uk/history-and-civilisation/2021/12/before-writing-little-women-louisa-may-alcott-penned-blood-and-thunder.

8. Sbardella, "Before Writing 'Little Women.'"

9. Anne Boyd Rioux, *Meg, Jo, Beth, Amy: The Story of Little Women and Why It Still Matters* (New York: Henry Holt, 2021), xiii.

10. Alcott, *Little Women*, 414, 419.

11. Alcott, *Little Women*, 414.

12. Alcott, *Little Women*, 415.

13. Rosie Colosi, "This Millennial Mortician Is Changing the Face of the Traditional Funeral Industry," MSNBC, October 16, 2019, https://www.msnbc.com/know-your-value/millennial-mortician-closing-casket-traditional-funeral-industry-n1067486.

14. Alcott, *Little Women*, 419.

15. As quoted in Andrew Solomon, "Under Pressure," *New York Times*, January 31, 2014, https://www.nytimes.com/2014/02/02/books/review/all-joy-and-no-fun-by-jennifer-senior.html.

16. Jennifer Senior, *All Joy and No Fun: The Paradox of Modern Parenthood* (New York: HarperCollins, 2014), 126–38.

17. Colosi, "This Millennial Mortician."

18. As quoted in Jennifer Luxton, "Breaking New Ground in the Mortuary Business," *The World*, February 18, 2018, https://theworld.org/stories/2016-05-06/what-does-feminist-mortician-look.

19. Alcott, *Little Women*, 419.

20. Emily Dickinson, "After great pain, a formal feeling comes— (372)," Poetry Foundation, accessed February 19, 2023, https://www.poetryfoundation.org/poems/47651/after-great-pain-a-formal-feeling-comes-372.

21. Amy Paturel, "The Traumatic Loss of a Loved One Is Like Experiencing a Brain Injury," *Discover*, August 7, 2020, https://www.discovermagazine.com/mind/the-traumatic-loss-of-a-loved-one-is-like-experiencing-a-brain-injury.

22. Harrington and Neimeyer, *Superhero Grief*, 19.

23. Harrington and Neimeyer, *Superhero Grief*, 51.

24. Harrington and Neimeyer, *Superhero Grief*, 51.

25. Harrington and Neimeyer, *Superhero Grief*, 53.

26. Harrington and Neimeyer, *Superhero Grief*, 52.

Chapter 13 Pansies for Faith

1. Elie Wiesel, *Night* (New York: Hill & Wang, 2006), 34.
2. Dara T. Mathis, "The Church's Black Exodus," *Atlantic*, October 11, 2020, https://www.theatlantic.com/politics/archive/2020/10/why-black-parishioners-are-leaving-churches/616588/.
3. Mathis, "Church's Black Exodus."
4. Kate Haynes Murphy, "NC Pastor: People Are Leaving Church—Because of Churches," *Charlotte Observer*, April 5, 2021, https://amp.charlotteobserver.com/opinion/article250389211.html.
5. Wiesel, *Night*, 34.
6. SparkNotes, "Night," SparkNotes, accessed February 20, 2023, https://www.sparknotes.com/lit/night/quotes/.
7. Elie Wiesel and Krista Tippett, "Elie Wiesel: The Tragedy of the Believer," *On Being*, July 13, 2006, https://onbeing.org/programs/elie-wiesel-the-tragedy-of-the-believer/.
8. Wiesel and Tippett, "Elie Wiesel."
9. Wiesel and Tippett, "Elie Wiesel."

Chapter 14 Passionflower for the Cross

1. Cahleen Shrier, "The Science of the Crucifixion," Azusa Pacific University, March 1, 2002, https://www.apu.edu/articles/the-science-of-the-crucifixion/#f3.
2. Shrier, "The Science of the Crucifixion."
3. Charles Haddon Spurgeon, "Lama Sabachthani?," The Spurgeon Center, February 18, 2023, https://www.spurgeon.org/resource-library/sermons/lama-sabachthani/#flipbook/.

Chapter 15 Ivy for the Burial

1. Wall text for "Vanitas Flower Still Life," by Willem van Aelst, 1656–57, oil on canvas, North Carolina Museum of Art, Raleigh, North Carolina.
2. Wall text for "Vanitas Flower Still Life," by Willem van Aelst.
3. Michael Petry, *Nature Morte: Contemporary Artists Reinvigorate the Still-Life Tradition* (New York: Thames & Hudson, 2013), 6.
4. Petry, *Nature Morte*, 6.
5. Petry, *Nature Morte*, 9.
6. Petry, *Nature Morte*, 9.
7. Cyrus Martin, "From Death Comes Life," *Current Biology*, February 22, 2023, https://www.sciencedirect.com/science/article/pii/S0960982216305954.
8. Jeannie Evers, "Bog," *National Geographic*, February 22, 2023, https://education.nationalgeographic.org/resource/bog/.
9. Richard Neitzel Holzapfel et al., "Jesus and the Ossuaries: First-Century Jewish Burial Practices and the Lost Tomb of Jesus," in *Behold the Lamb of God: An Easter Celebration*, edited by Richard Neitzel Holzapfel, Frank F. Judd Jr., and Thomas A. Wayment (Provo, UT: Religious Studies Center, 2008), 201–36.
10. "Strong's G142: airō," Blue Letter Bible, accessed June 21, 2023, https://www.blueletterbible.org/lexicon/g142/niv/mgnt/0-1/.

11. Martin, "From Death Comes Life."

12. Ira Loucks, "Fungi from the Biblical Perspective: Design and Purpose in the Original Creation," *Answers Research Journal* 2 (2009): 123–31, https://answersresearch journal.org/fungi-from-the-biblical-perspective/.

Chapter 16 Lily of the Valley for New Life

1. Henry M. Morris, "The God of Heaven," *Days of Praise*, April 28, 2015, https://www.icr.org/article/8595.

2. Mara Johnson-Groh, "What If the Moon Disappeared Tomorrow?," *Astronomy*, November 25, 2019, https://www.astronomy.com/science/what-if-the-moon-disappeared-tomorrow/.

3. Pieter G. R. de Villiers, "The Resurrection as Christ's Entry into His Glory (Lk. 24:26)," *Acta Theologica* 31, suppl. 15 (January 2011): 101–31, http://www.scielo.org.za/scielo.php?script=sci_arttext&pid=S1015-87582011000400010&lng=en&nrm=iso.

ABOUT RACHEL

Rachel Marie Kang is the author of *Let There Be Art* and founder of The Fallow House. She is a New York native, born and raised just outside New York City, and a mixed woman of African American, Native American (Ramapough Lenape Nation), Irish, and Dutch descent. Rachel holds a degree in English with creative writing and a minor in Bible. Her work has been featured in *Christianity Today*, Ekstasis, Proverbs 31 Ministries, She Reads Truth, and (in)courage. She lives in North Carolina with her husband and two children.

Connect with Rachel

I'd love to connect and keep in touch with you. Visit my website to find inspiration for your faith and creativity, receive updates on my work and writing, and read a free chapter of my first book, *Let There Be Art*.

RachelMarieKang.com

 @RachelMarieKang

@RachelMarieKang

@RachelMarieKang